fə

67

ONE DAY OF LIFE
IS LIFE

JOAN MARAGALL

TRANSLATION AND EDITION BY RONALD PUPPO

PREFACE BY MICHAEL EAUDE

FUM D'ESTAMPA PRESS LTD.
LONDON - BARCELONA

This translation has been published in Great Britain
by Fum d'Estampa Press Limited 2020

001

Translation copyright © Ronald Puppo, 2019
Preface copyright © Michael Eaude, 2020

The moral right of the author and translator has been asserted
Set in Minion Pro

Printed and bound by TJ Books Limited, Padstow, Cornwall
A CIP catalogue record for this book is available from the British Library

ISBN: 978-1-9162939-5-3

Series design by 'el mestre' Rai Benach

All rights reserved.
This book is sold subject to the condition that it shall not,
by way of trade or otherwise, be lent, resold, hired out or
otherwise circulated without the publisher's prior consent
in any form of binding or cover other than that in which it
is published and without a similar condition including this
condition being imposed on the subsequent purchaser.

This work was translated with the help of a grant from the Institut Ramon Llull.

**institut
ramon llull**
Catalan Language and Culture

FUM D'ESTAMPA PRESS

CONTENTS

- PROSE -

LAVA
PREFACE BY MICHAEL EAUDE

It is no accident that the brave group of anti-Franco protesters sang Joan Maragall's *Song to the Catalan Flag* (see p. 124) in Barcelona's Palau de la Música Catalana on 19 May 1960. Organised by Cristians Catalans, this famous event was the moment conservative Catalan nationalism was reborn in public, twenty years after the Spanish Civil War defeat. It led to a seven-year prison sentence (of which he served just three and a half) for Jordi Pujol, President (1980-2003) of the Generalitat, Catalonia's autonomous government. Maragall was a key historical reference for the protesters: he was a Catholic and Catalan nationalist, and someone of profound religiosity who yet fought to renew the church and the society it dominated.

In his day, Maragall was better known as author of some 400-plus articles in the conservative press than for his passionate, radical poetry. His best-known article, suppressed for twenty years (*City of Pardon*, see p. 237), comes late in his short life. Not at all conservative, it pleads for clemency after the 1909 Setmana Tràgica uprising. In the name of love and religious awe before the beautiful complexity of a human body, he speaks out against vengeance and for understanding of those condemned. This, he believed, could turn Barcelona from the "city of bombs" to a "city of pardon." The Setmana Tràgica opened what is a constant fracture in the Church: the mechanical, complacent ritual of the hierarchy as opposed to the church of love, exalted by Maragall in the articles featured in this selection. He found primitive beauty in a Mass held in a burnt-out church. The protesters in 1960 saw themselves as living a similar struggle: against Franco's brutal National-Catholicism and for a church that would break with dictatorship and executions.

Maragall was arguing for social responsibility. Though he, like the textile magnates of Catalonia's industrial revolution, feared and loathed the rise of the anarchists, he opposed the blanket repression that Enric Prat de la Riba, leader of the Lliga Regionalista, deman-ded from the Spanish state. Maragall believed that society had to tackle the unbearable social conditions that underlay revolts like the Setmana Tràgica. The anarchists, he thought, could be defeated by creating a more just society.

Like many artistic-minded upper-class young men he had des-pised conventional work, but his father's failed investments in 1886 meant he had to work as a lawyer to support the family. In 1890 he changed direction, becoming secretary to the editor of the *Diario de Barcelona*. He soon began to write articles, introducing *moder-nista* ideas into this conservative paper. *Modernisme* (or Catalan *Art nouveau*) was the movement of the 1890s and first decade of the twentieth century that aimed to renew both culture and society. Its ideologues had been born, like Maragall or the painter and writer Santiago Rusiñol, into the first wave of the *Renaixença*, the rebirth making Catalan the language of culture, not just the vernacular. The second-wave generation toward the end of the century was more political. These *modernista* artists, of whom Maragall was the outstanding literary figure, wanted to transform their oppressed nation by recovering mediaeval traditions and modernizing the country. They and Catalonia's new bourgeoisie aspired to lead a more forward-moving Spain, not to separate from it.

Maragall took part in the art jamborees organized by Rusiñol in Sitges in 1892-94, which celebrated the latest ideas from Europe. He had taught himself German by studying Goethe and read excerpts from Nietzsche at the 1892 festival. Later he distanced himself from this more bohemian current. No *poète maudit*, he became a refined patriarch, though his open character meant that he was not one to sever relations with people who thought differently. Indeed, in the first decade of the twentieth century, the afternoon teas hosted by his English wife Clara Noble (mother of his 13 children) united politicians, artists, and writers of varying ideologies. Even the prickly architect Antoni Gaudí sometimes attended. Maragall's friendship with Gaudí is illuminating, for the latter believed that religion was all about self-denial and suffering. The Sagrada Família was being built to expiate the atheist anarchists' sins. Maragall was much milder. In his art, too, he was something of an anti-Gaudí, in that he was no fan of over-embellishment, quite unlike Gaudí's baroque buildings of twisting brick. Maragall sought the simplicity of spoken language. I am talking about his startlingly direct poetry, not his conventionally flowery prose: *Ah! Barcelona...* (see page 232) has a 14-line opening sentence!

Maragall's poetry is a revelation, both accessible and subtle. There is nothing I can add to Ronald Puppo's erudite introductions, except to join him in wonder at the poems. Maragall was a poet of freedom in nature, of joy in life. His framework is religious, but not limited. After witnessing the barbaric slaughter of the 1893 Liceu bomb, he celebrates his baby daughter's innocence expressed in her "barbaric laugh." In the excerpt from *Count Arnau*, he poses simply the choice faced by the Abbess either of being wedded to Christ or using her "fleshy lips" to kiss the Count. The famous *Ode to Spain* (1898) rejects old, imperial Spain's cult of death. In *The End of Serra-llonga*, he sings the outlaw's lust for life: sex with his beloved Joana cannot be sinful, as the priest would have it. The calm, reasonable Maragall is a poet of flesh and feeling. Read him and find, as the writer Gaziel put it, that "under the carpet of a meadow in spring…, lava was running through the depths."

Michael Eaude

INTRODUCTION

We understand each other only through the love of words.
—Joan Maragall

I had never seen, before visiting Barcelona, a poster with the words *Estima la teva llengua* / Love your language. Spain's diverse cultures and language communities are often met with indifference, ignorance, or even disdain. That said, the nineteenth and early twentieth-century burst of vitality signaling Catalan's road to recovery throws into relief not only the voices of the poets and writers captaining the literary landscape, but also those given voice by these voices. The poster, whose statement may prove puzzling to speakers of mainstream global languages, gives proof of the uncanny resilience of a distinct language community, their love of the word and its indissoluble link to life, and the ongoing shared delight, and pain, in struggling to safeguard both—the word and the common life—against all historical odds.

Joan Maragall's groundbreaking poetry, disarmingly uncomplex on the surface, encapsulates both the turbulence of his time and place (the anarchist bomb attack in the Barcelona Liceu Opera

House, the spiritual cost of the Spanish-American War, the social meltdown of Barcelona's 1909 Tragic Week) and the serenity of his gaze into world and soul. Maragall's late-life landmark poem "Cant espiritual" ("Spiritual") caught the eye of Albert Camus (1913-1960) and Eugenio Montale (1896-1981), whose French and Italian translations of this heartfelt agnostic prayer poem appeared in 1957 and 1975, and his steadfast friendship with Miguel de Unamuno (1864-1936) brings to light their disagreement on how Catalan society might help put Spain back on democratic track: for Unamuno, this must be accomplished through the Spanish language; for Maragall, Catalan could not be sacrificed—a position powerfully articulated in Maragall's 1910 reply to José Ortega y Gasset (1883-1955), "*La verdadera cuestión previa,*" (included in this selection).

In the framework of literary and artistic periods, Maragall emerges as the outstanding poet of Catalan modernism—Modernisme. Paralleling Maragall's poetic achievement during the Modernisme period are, among others, novelists Raimon Casellas (1855-1910), Prudenci Bertrana (1867-1941), and Caterina Albert (aka Víctor Català, 1869-1966); painters Santiago Rusiñol (1861-1931) and Ramon Casas (1866-1932); and architects Lluís Domènech i Montaner (1849-1923) and, most famously, Antoni Gaudí (1852-1926). Alongside his poetic production, however, Maragall's prolific and incisive writing as a columnist for Barcelona's most influential newspapers earned him a widely respected reputation as he weighed in on matters social, political and literary; Maragall's commitment to rigorous engagement in the debates of his day—his articles and other prose texts amount to well over four hundred writings—impacts powerfully on the depth and breadth of Maragall's perspective and contribution, cutting an emerging figure of prototype for the twentieth-century *intellectuel engagé* not unlike Émile Zola (1840-

1902) (see Terricabras 2011; Torrents 2011, 315; and in particular, Maragall's three articles on the Tragic Week included in this selection). Writing poetry in Catalan and penning his soul-searching analyses of the troubles of his day in both Catalan and Spanish (varying with publishing outlet or readership), Maragall emerged as a powerful voice, reacting always with a clear and strong commitment to conviviality and civic purpose. On Maragall's standing within the broader Spanish borders, the late Arthur Terry (1927-2004) has written:

[Maragall] achieved a quite remarkable authority, both through his unremitting honesty as a journalist and a public figure, and through his correspondence and friendships with Castilian writers like Giner de los Ríos, Unamuno and Azorín. (Terry 2003, 81)

Hailed by Aragonese writer and former president of the Real Academia Española, Pedro Laín Entralgo (1908-2001), as the "primogenitor of the Generación del 98" (Laín 1960, 26), Maragall is nevertheless aware that in choosing his native Catalan as vehicle for literary expression, he may be perceived in some quarters as a divisive element. In a hegemonic mindset where European nation-states have gravitated toward monolingual institutions, the taking of second-tier or unofficial languages too seriously may be seen as an affront, or even a threat, to the official language of a sovereign state and its preferential language community. Maragall makes it clear that his defense of linguistic pluralism goes hand-in-hand with intercultural conviviality:

Let us keep in mind that we are not rebels waving one flag against another flag [...] Our cause is not only that of our own nation, nor is it a stately dispute or family feud. It is a matter of a human ideal rooted in the divine love that so beautifully vitalizes the world. (Maragall [1903] 1960, 666-667)

It is Christian ethics—the notion of universal love—that comes into play here with the acceptance of linguistic and cultural plurality. Further, as a reflection of the diversity in nature itself, linguistic diversity gains legitimacy in the context of a Christian cosmology in which embracing diversity is to embrace the divine plan.

One Day of Life is Life

Maragall's poetry is an affirmation and celebration of life in the face of life's many adversaries. Even death, understood as the inevitable outcome of every life, pales beside the living of a life. Living fully, however, requires engaging the moment at every moment: "Dare the moment; / dare the moment inviting, / and you'll spring with gusto into every combat; / one day of life is life: / dare the moment given you. // Don't grieve, then, these funeral Novembers, / nor lament the death of that which fully was... / Lament the young who put their limbs to rest / without first having tired them in delight" ("November Song"). Perhaps not unlike as in W.B. Yeats' (1865-1939) "lonely impulse of delight" ("An Irish Airman Foresees His Death"), we sense that the impulse daring the moment is both organic and spiritual; Maragall consistently and stubbornly resists detaching spiritual life from the worldly (see in particular: "The End of Serrallonga" and "Spiritual"). The spirit of each individual person, we might say, is tasked with keeping the impulse activated throughout one's whole life: "Keep watch, spirit, keep watch, / keep your compass to your star; / beware being drawn to the calm / subdued waters of harbors" ("Excelsior").

"Non-Taxable Roses" depicts the triumph of life over another of life's adversaries—unfreedom. Swaying high on a garden wall, beyond reach, these roses "know no servitude, […] no brazen hand will bouquet them, / no human breath will taint them." The portrayal of the ideal freedom enjoyed by the non-taxable roses stands in illustrative contrast to the somber unfreedom of the factory-working family in "The Siren," recalling other examples of social poetry by Maragall's near-contemporaries on the Iberian peninsula; notably, Rosalía de Castro (1837-1885) in poems such as "Tembra un neno no húmedo pórtico" (*Follas novas* III, 41) and "A xusticia pola man" (*FN* II, 25); and also Jacint Verdaguer's (1845-1902) "Per què canten les mares" and "La boira" (*Caritat*) (see Puppo 2017, 347-348, 353). In "Ash Wednesday: To a Young Woman" the unfreedom to be confronted is that of dogma, or dogmatic ritual, which works to undermine the joy of living: "Stay clear of those ashes, stay away from the ashes, / custodian of youth, / death and ashes, you know, haven't the least bit to do with you. / Don't let this token tarnish / your forehead rosy and fresh." In this strikingly irreverent poem (Maragall was, we recall, a devout Catholic) the ritual remembrance of death has no place in the living of a life, not even for one day.

Maragall speaks to a more subtle adversary of life in "The Beech Woods of Jordà," namely, the self-limitation by which we fence in our living, dulling our senses, and devitalizing our capacity to perceive and engage the world. In a way that is reminiscent of a Rousseaunian reverie, the solitary walker reaches a spot deep in the woods where a "sweet oblivion of the world takes hold," and amid the overwhelming green stillness, an uncanny sensation of living freedom washes over the walker, a feeling of "fellowship" with the "liberating prison" that are the woods. A somewhat more elaborate blending of self with the natural world is recounted in "The Mountains," drawing to a climactic conclusion in which Maragall, as elsewhere, resists the material–spiritual dichotomy while at the same time distancing himself from pantheism, embracing rather a pananthropism (Serrahima 1981, 106) coupled with the fruition of the mind and the senses in the natural world. In the poem following, "Return," the poet returns to a self once again separate from the world, given the brevity of the coalescence, and the human spirit must once again confront the world in the search for meaning, and freedom, by means of reflection and action. No longer does the self blend with the world, it must now engage it.

In the trilogy *Three Songs of War* ("The Good-byes," "Ode to Spain" and "Song of Return"), Maragall powerfully combines the office of poet with that of turn-of-the-century *intellectuel engagé*. It is now the degradation of the common life that—with the disastrous prolongation and eventual collapse of Spanish colonialism in Cuba, Puerto Rico and the Philippines—emerges here as the enemy of living. The first poem, "The Good-byes," stands as a forceful rebuttal to war and violence that is all the more astonishing for its brevity. In the second, "Ode to Spain," Maragall admonishes Mother Spain for her inability, or unwillingness, to reject violence and death—"and funerals were your festivals, / sad Spain"—and embrace her own children in all their rich diversity; echoing, by the way, Rosalía de Castro's "A gaita gallega" (*Cantares gallegos*) and its unequivocal affirmation of Galician identity distinct from that imposed by Spanish politico-economic and administrative centralism. In the remarkable poem closing the trilogy, "Song of Return," the dramatic upturn and revitalization in the poem's conclusion signals the revitalization of the land, the word, and the common life. It is also the degradation of the common life that Maragall addresses in his bold and brilliant "New Ode to Barcelona," through which, together with his three articles penned amid the profound social strife concomitant to the Setmana

Tràgica, or Tragic Week of 1909 ("Ah! Barcelona…," "City of Pardon" and "The Church After Burning;" included in this selection), Maragall challenges his fellow citizens to examine their consciences and put into practice the Christian-inspired, public-spirited love that, in Maragall's view, is so crucial to conviviality.

In the extraordinary poems "The End of Serrallonga," "Sunstruck" and "Spiritual" the adversary of life which Maragall confronts is none other than the Christian dogma driving an existential wedge between worldly life and spiritual life. On the surface, "The End of Serrallonga" showcases the popular seventeenth-century Catalan outlaw's day of reckoning, serving as entry point into reflection on a life of sin. Embedded in the poem's concluding lines, however, as Abrams (2010, 145) convincingly spotlights, is the outlaw's refusal to embrace a posthumous spiritual life severed from worldly life; of course, it is the seeds of Maragall's own existential query that are at work here, subsequently spelled out in his renowned late-life poem "Spiritual." In his masterly parable "Sunstruck," Maragall serves up an empowering alternative to the tragic scenario played out in Caterina Albert's *La infanticida* (1898) (*The infanticide*, translation by Kathleen McNerney, 2018); Maragall's brilliant fable-like portrayal of single-mother pregnancy embraces and celebrates birth and life in the face of the destructive stigma of dogmatic taboo. Finally, in his renowned masterpiece, the prayer poem "Spiritual," the poet struggles in earnest to reconcile the existential gap between immanence and transcendence; here again, Maragall is reluctant to embrace a spiritual life severed from worldly life.

Maragall's Living Word

In his 1903 address titled *Elogi de la paraula* (In Praise of Words), delivered at Barcelona's iconic culture and arts club founded in 1860, the Ateneu Barcelonès, Maragall formulated his views on poetry and the power of words around the notion of the "living word." Later, in his 1907 essay *Elogi de la poesia* (In Praise of Poetry), he developed his ideas further—examining the question of whether poetic lines should be subject to traditional constraints or, by contrast, display variation, spontaneity, simplicity and sincerity over constraining templates, lexical and syntactic complexity, and the elaborate outward forms of his Romantic predecessors. Maragall's plea for leveling the wall between ordinary speech and poetry springs from the very mystery of speech and words themselves, and our understanding of them, in three interconnected ways. First, there is the sacred quality of words in the Christian cosmology and theology that nurtured Maragall's spiritual life since his childhood. Second, there is the natural and powerful human drive to give expression to experiences and ideas through words, that is, a sanctity of words in a worldly sense. Finally, there is the notion of the "living word," in which the wonder and power of speech stems from the speaker's receptivity to sensations giving rise to poetic expression, as Maragall put it, "stirring to spiritual life an entire world within us" (Maragall [1903b] 1960, 663; this and all subsequent translations from the Catalan are mine).

The sacred quality of speech as understood in its most literal Judeo–Christian sense—the Word—adds authority, a sort of biblical seal of approval, to Maragall's theoretical construct. In the second and more secular sense, the sanctity of words is relocated into the realm of human experience, now lowercased, but still a source of power and wonder:

[Words] bring together and blend all of Nature's bodily and spiritual marvels. It is as if the earth mustered all its strength to bring forth men and women as the utmost meaningful product it might give; and as if men and women, in turn, mustered all the strength of their being to give words. (663)

Needless to say, this sense of the power and wonder of words wears away with the proliferation of verbal exchange, in which "the habit of too much talking and too much listening muddles our sense of the sanctity of words" (663). With a view to regaining a sense of the power and wonder of words, Maragall invites us to recall those occasions which tap feelings deep within us: "Have you never walked deep in woods and felt the serene fullness of life akin to wondering at all the earth?" Or take the speech of lovers, whose "words are like blossoms [and before] love speaks, how life stirs in all the branches of its senses!" (664)

It is precisely this freshly renewed receptivity to sensations, jump-started by our encounters with the world and with others, that can put the power and wonder back into words. Poets, Maragall remarks, speak like lovers. "They are the lovers of all in the world [looking] at everything as if under a spell [and speaking] a word that creates; not unlike God's handiwork the first day in Genesis, from chaos comes the light." Addressing the poets in the audience at his 1903 speech, he asks: "When will you search deep down into your souls to hear only its divine rhythm pulsing with love for the things of the earth? When will you block out all other rhythms and speak only in living words?" Maragall is unequivocal in his defense of what he calls the living word:

But now, unhappily, you would often take an ounce of inspiration and try to raise buildings fraught with self-importance, foolishly inflating your rhythms and filling them with words that float lifeless on the surface of things. So people tire of your vain tedium and your dull music, and take you for laborious oddballs, which is what you are. When you happened on a word that might light up the world, your itching for shallow perfection and grandeur enveloped it in a swarming cloud of lifeless words that dimmed the light divine, relegating it once again to the shadows. (664-665)

So, in sharp contrast to a poetics of cosmopolitan-bred sophistication, Maragall prescribes a model of earthy simplicity and receptivity:

Learn to speak from the people: not from the self-important people you seek to impress with your self-important words, but rather the people of simple living [...] Learn from shepherds and mariners. What gift they have for gazing at the world's majesty, where the spirit throbs in free and boundless tempo! What vastness mirrored in their eyes [...] What fragrant and salty seas and fresh fields, what pure sensations touch their hearts! Their features lack sophistication and they rarely speak, but when they do their words ring clear with meaning. (665)

Maragall's notion that the force of language is rooted in "the people" can be understood on two levels, each based on separate but interrelated definitions of the word "people," and Maragall points to the importance of both. In the first sense, as above, we understand "the people" as the common or ordinary members of a particular society (the definite article fuel-injects this sense into the noun), and we speak of "the people" in contrast to, say, "the elite" or "the ruling class." The speech of the people, Maragall argues, is spontaneous and natural—born, as he puts it, "in the rhythmic pulsating of the universe" which, if we are to grasp it, requires that we carefully adjust our sensors. The unfiltered utterances of Maragall's shepherds and mariners are the stuff of living language; the poet's task is to follow suit, articulating sensory input in a language as simple and sublime as the raw sensations themselves, now simply and effectively packaged into living words. For Maragall, once poets have shown us this sublime language,

Their kingdom will come and everyone will speak under the spell of their creative music. We will all speak as in song, each of our voices issuing from the earth, putting aside the artifice of conventional language, getting through to each other [...] we will get through to all who listen under its spell [...] This only is universal language. (665-666)

Of course, this universal language is expressed, in actual practice, through concrete and particular languages. This is where Maragall brings in the notion of "people" in a crucial second sense: separate from but inextricably interwoven with the first sense: "The only universal speech," writes Maragall, "is that manifold speech which is as varied as the multiple varieties of lands and their peoples" (666). Just as the final "s" added to "people" designates cultural plurality, activating a wide-angle lens where linguistic and cultural diversity shift into view, Maragall, too, designates cultural and linguistic plurality as a natural and desirable state of affairs: "what other arrangement of peoples and lands should be aspired to other than that which has sprung from the spontaneous life of their languages?" Maragall understands his acceptance of plurality as consistent with his notion of the sanctity of speech:

It is obvious, then, that our cause is a good one, and taking into account that it stems from the divine mystery of being and becoming, and that it stands above all conventional politics and historical contingencies, we will defend it gladly and devotedly, bringing to our struggle a greatness that will safeguard it from egoism and ill-will, far from the reach of short-sighted self-interest, whether our own or in others. (666)

As poetized brilliantly in "Song of Return," Maragall voices the re-vitalization of his own particular language—and its people—in the context of a distinct language community and its struggle to carry forward the living word and the common life. Reflecting on the significance of the language of the people being rooted in the living word of the people, Francesc Parcerisas has observed that Maragall's is not a vindication of the language as such, but rather "a vindication of the authenticity of the word of the people" (Parcerisas 2012, 455).

Overstating the enormity of Maragall's insight into the impor-tance of language, and of languages, would not be easy. In his incisive study of Maragall's poetry and poetics, Lluís Solà has pointed out that "we do not stand outside of language;" it is, as Ramon Llull (1232-1316) observed long ago, humankind's sixth sense (Solà 2013, 57). We might say that alongside space and time (the Kantian a priori forms of sensible intuition) there stands language, which, far from being a mere instrument, is the very substance that opens the way to relations with others, the world, history—past, present and future—and, not least of all, ourselves (56-57). To lose sight of this would be to cut short the life of words.

A Population or a People?

We have seen how it was the degradation of the common life that impelled Maragall to pen his remarkable Tragic Week articles in which he challenged his fellow citizens to rise above the hypocrisy, scapegoating, and widespread high-handed repression that took hold in the wake of the fatal events that struck the heart of Catalan society during the week of 26-31 July 1909. Particularly striking in the first of his three post-Tragic Week articles, "Ah! Barcelona…," is the discursive place given to the notion of love, which in Maragall constitutes the moral core of his urgent appeal to the population. Perhaps even more striking is the prominence of this Christian-inspired, public-spirited love in Maragall's view of a convivial society: it is precisely because recourse to law and order, or even civil or religious authority has failed to put things right that the notion of love emerges in Maragall as the highest social value, causing him to identify love as the "primary social reason." Maragall's response is that the population must itself come up with a response: a public-spirited love whose lacking points to not only the absence of Christian purpose but also the absence of social purpose. Love, Maragall concludes, is the "mettle of peoples,"—the catalyst that converts a mere population into a people. Finally, alerting his readers that there can be no love without suffering, Maragall urges Barcelona to seek out its own grief, and "those who want no part of it, let them leave." Then, concluding the article by sketching a worst-case scenario in the hope of nudging his readers into reflection and action, Maragall continues:

And if in the end everyone has gone, the traveler gazing out at Barcelona and Catalonia, deserted and desolate, might say: Here there may have been a great population, but there certainly never was a people.

Although in this first article Maragall cannot say exactly what kind of love must take hold, in the second one, "City of Pardon," the love marshaling reflection and action must be directed toward that before which they have thrown up a wall of indifference: the city's wrong-doers and scapegoats facing military tribunals and death sentences. There can be no redemption for the city without love, nor can there be love without the painful act of reconciliation. Known at that time as the "city of bombs," Barcelona might—should Maragall's appeal for clemency prove fruitful—take on a new name: "city of pardon." In his third article, "The Church After Burning," Maragall calls on his readers to interrogate themselves about the true meaning of their Christian faith. Maragall was adamant in taking aim both at the anticlerical violence in Barcelona the previous July and the hypocrisy of the city's more sanctimonious churchgoers, as well as faulting the Church for alienating the poor, and calling into question the virtue of the city's wealthy: "If Christ were to walk again among men, surely those to count themselves among His followers would be they, not you" (see Lluís Font 2009). For Maragall, social renewal was only possible through regeneration of the spirit, the lack of which exposed a Christian faith that had degenerated into static class-inscribed ritual; and a Barcelona that, for all its population, had been un-peopled. Just as the power of language is to be found in living words, the power of Christian values is to be found in a living faith.

Topping off the Tragic Week articles is Maragall's poetized call for social and spiritual renewal in his extraordinary "New Ode to Barcelona," whose depths can be effectively sounded when read in tandem with these articles. The rich semantics of "New" in the poem's title references Maragall's Romantic predecessor Jacint Verdaguer's equally extraordinary ode "To Barcelona" while signaling the need for spiritual and social renewal (given voice, we might add, by a renewed poetics). The spiritual renewal is powerfully symbolized in the poem by the emergence of architect Antoni Gaudí's new Holy Family Temple (in contrast to the role of Barcelona Cathedral in Verdaguer's poem); and with the return to a living faith—spiritual renewal—comes the turn from population to people. The new temple and new spiritual and social landscape call to mind the adroit appearance of the figure of the shepherdess whose new song brings redemption to the condemned count at the very end of *Count Arnau* (part three).

The central role of living—and life-giving—words in Maragall brings to mind again his 1903 address, *In Praise of Words*, which, we might note, was delivered only months after Spain's royal decree (21 November 1902) which forbade teaching in Catalan (and Euskera and Galician) under threat of the loss of teaching credentials and loss of "all the rights recognized by the law" (see Resina 2009, 32n). The decree was a high-handed move to suppress the gathering empowerment of Spain's diverse language communities; Maragall's groundbreaking poetry and prose contributed to their advancement in no small way. In voicing, and giving voice to, a people and their love of the word and its indissoluble link to life, Maragall stands tall in the struggle to safeguard the word and the common life against all historical odds.

The Translation

I have undertaken the task of bringing Maragall to English-language readers by observing as far as possible Friedrich Schleiermacher's (1768-1834) seminal insight (Schleiermacher [1813] 2004); to wit, by also bringing English-language readers to Maragall with the aid of contextual essentials to help transport readers to the time and place in which the fin-de-siècle Catalan poet and writer's voice emerged. This means acquainting readers not only with Maragall's poetry and prose, but also his poetics, his place in the literary and artistic movements of his day—in particular, Modernisme—and the peculiar circumstance of the growing empowerment of diverse language communities within Spain's variegated cultural and linguistic fabric. Where the texts themselves are concerned, we have followed Maragall's own dictum of leveling the wall between ordinary speech and poetry, emulating his simplicity and clarity of expression.

Among the thousands of lexical, syntactic, rhythmic, and pragmatic choices made in the process of Englishing Maragall's poems in this volume, myriad could be used to illustrate how inter-linguistic and intercultural transference must inevitably pass through an array of filters of language and cultural difference. Let us look at a few examples. In the poem "La vaca cega" ("The Cow Gone Blind"), attempting to recreate the title in English by way of a lexical calque, "the blind cow," leads to a syntactic impasse: it is rhetorically ineffec-tive because the terms are reversed; whereas in the original Catalan the theme precedes the rheme, reversing the order to comply with English syntax proves anticlimactic. In the Catalan title, first comes the animal and then the animal's blindness, paralleling the sequence of events in the poem itself. The cow had not always been blind. The disturbing sensation that is so central to this poem is subtly woven into the poem's expository logic. Preserving and recasting that logic in translating the title might be achieved by reproducing the theme–rheme pattern with an English title such as "The Cow Gone Blind." Elsewhere in the same poem, my first attempts at verbalizing in English the image of the "film that set in the other eye" ("en l'altre / se li ha posat un tel") did not sound very satisfying to me; then I made a connection, an intertextual correspondence—the description of a cat, blind in one eye, that leapt out at me from the page (the description, not the cat) as I happened to be rereading Truman Capote's (1924-1984) *Breakfast at Tiffany's*. Here is part of Capote's description of the animal: "it was a grim cat with a pirate's cutthroat face; one eye was gluey-blind, the other sparkled with dark deeds" (Capote 1993, 34). So, honing my lines with the addition of "gluey"—"a gluey film / has claimed her sight in the other"—I was now satisfied with the semantic and rhythmic result. One of the thorniest lexical decisions to be made arose at the end of "Fatherhood," where the Catalan "riu bàrbarament" might be translated either as "lets go a barbaric laugh" or "lets go a barbarous laugh." To allude or not to allude, that was the issue. Separately, but still in connection with this, Maragall's enthusiasm for Nietzschean vitalism at the time he wrote this poem is, as more than one critic have pointed out, a key element here, as is the connection between the "innocent child" in the poem and that of *Also sprach Zarathustra*, fragments of which Maragall had translated (Abrams 2010, 56-59; Casals 1998, 134-135). The Whitman-evoking resonance of "barbaric," then, in this final climactic line, seems to me entirely consistent with the poem's vitalist and tradition-breaking character. Finally, testing the bounds of what Peter Bush (2006) has called "writerly decisions," I have rendered the Catalan "Adéu, Espanya!" verbatim—an exoticism—in the final line of "Ode to Spain." Here, the problem of making visible to non-Iberian readers the barrier between preferential and peripheral language communities within Spain is compounded by what Lawrence Venuti has described as "the violence of translating: the sheer loss of the multiple contexts in which the foreign work originated and which always inform the foreign reader's experience of it" (Venuti 2009, XVII-XVIII). To even begin to render an appreciation of the intercultural subtext that informs the Catalan reader's experience of the poem, linguistic transference in terms of lexico-semantic equivalence will not be enough; as Gayatri Chakravorty Spivak reminds us: "it is not bodies of meaning that are transferred in translation," but rather an *other* that is transferred (Spivak 1993, 179). Translation is more than simple communication (perhaps a rather devitalized notion)—it is encounter. To encounter a cultural other—and more especially, as in this case, a cultural other struggling to safeguard the word and the common life—we must attempt to step outside our own cultural safety zone. One way of doing this is by using exoticisms, that is, the verbatim transfer of foreign words into a translated text. It should be noted here that this is a well-known feature of countless literary texts even in their original, untranslated forms: from Geoffrey Chaucer and William Shakespeare to Rudyard Kipling, Kate Chopin, T. S. Eliot, Alan Paton and Toni Morrison, writers have used Latinisms, Gallicisms, Italianisms, Indianisms, Afrikaansisms, Bantuisms and many more to transport readers to new spheres of cultural encounter. Why should translation preclude the use of such an effective writing technique? In an earlier rendering of Maragall's "Oda a Espanya," translator Mary Ann Newman takes an important step in this direction, translating the final line: Farewell, Espanya!, which confronts English readers with the Catalan toponym, making for an unfamiliar rhetoricity that nudges them closer to encountering the other. I have simply taken this strategy a step further, serving up verbatim the other half of the hard-hitting final line as well: Adéu, Espanya!

Maragall's meter and rhyme combine into a balanced composition of uncanny innovative and traditional elements. Many of these, and their various effects in the workings of the poems, are annotated and examined in detail in the endnotes of this volume. Maragall's varying meter, clashes in rhyme, and on occasion his use of unpaired verses in the original Catalan may, at times, signal an important moment in a poem, as in, for instance, the unpaired verses "Moriré resant el credo" in the closing lines of "The End of Serrallonga" and "aixequem una Senyera" in "Song to the Catalan Flag" (see endnotes); similarly, the rich blend of varying meter in *Count Arnau* (part two) counterpoints the shifting perspectives in the exchange between the Poet and Adalaisa (see endnotes). In rendering Maragall's adroit form–content synthesis into English verse it has not always been possible, and in some cases, I would say, not desirable, to reproduce the Catalan end rhyme; nor is Catalan meter directly transferable into English. As in my earlier encounter with Jacint Verdaguer (2007; 2015), rendering Maragall into rhythmic, readable, modern English verse has meant re-creating an appropriate form–content synthesis through the use of rhythmic elements such as weak rhyme, internal rhyme, slant rhyme, assonance, alliteration and the reworking of meter and rhythm; most of all, it means reading and rereading the texts—aloud—and making the "hundred visions and revisions" requisite to poking and prodding Maragall's living word out of its new shell.

I am again deeply indebted to a number of specialists who have opened many avenues along the way of my exploring Maragall over the past decade. Particularly invaluable has been the generous guidance and support of my accomplished colleagues in Vic: Ricard Torrents, Francesc Codina, Ramon Pinyol, M. Àngels Verdaguer, and distinguished poet Lluís Solà; in Figueres, eye-opening lectures by Margarida Casacuberta, Àngels Gardella, and Lourdes Godoy, with the support of Lluís Casadellà and Dolors Cunillera, have provided me with many insights; and in Barcelona, prominent Maragall scholars Glòria Casals, Francesco Ardolino, Josep M. Jaumà, and Ignasi Moreta; and also in Barcelona, I gleaned gold from my conversations with distinguished poet Enric Casasses. Thanks to the generosity of all, I have come to feel like the dwarf on the shoulders of giants. My heartfelt thanks to publisher Douglas Suttle for championing my translation of Maragall. I am especially indebted to the guidance, support, and steadfast friendship of Pere Maragall and Núria Aguirre, to whom this volume is dedicated.

I gràcies, Teresa… també estimo la teva llengua.

CHRONOLOGY

1860

Birth of Joan Maragall i Gorina, fourth and last child, and only son, of Josep Maragall Vilarosal and Rosa Gorina Folch, at number 4 Carrer Jaume Giralt in Barcelona on 10 October.

1875

According to Maragall's autobiographical notes, his period of childhood happiness comes to an end a year before completing his secondary schooling. Writes poetry abundantly. Begins an apprenticeship in his father's textile factory.

1877

Travels to Valencia, Granada, Córdoba, Madrid and Saragossa in January; Marseille and Paris in the summer.

1878

First known publication, the poem "Òptica" in the political and literary weekly *Lo Nunci*.

1879

Leaves the job at his father's factory and begins studying law at the Universitat de Barcelona. Later writes that now began a new period of youthful happiness.

1881

Confides his admiration for German literature, Goethe's *Werther* in particular, and declares himself an "enthusiast of Catalanism." Reads also Goethe's *Faust* and *Hermann and Dorothea*, Dickens's *Barnaby Rudge*, several cantos of Dante's *Divine Comedy*, Chateaubriand's *René*, and Víctor Balaguer's *Recuerdos de viaje*. Plays Verdi's *Aida*, Boito's *Mefistofele* and other works on the piano "a couple of hours a day." Submits the poem "Dins sa cambra" in Barcelona's Jocs Florals and wins a prize.

1882

Begins studying German with a private tutor, continuing for two years until taking his law degree.

1883

Sees the young woman Amanda at the Liceu and admires her from afar; confides his love for her in a letter to friend Josep M. Lloret.

1884

Graduates in law from the Universitat de Barcelona. Acquires the complete works of Goethe in German. Finds work clerking with an attorney.

1885

Summer sojourn at Cornellà, where he translates Goethe, returning frequently to Barcelona on job-related visits. Turns twenty-five (legal age) and begins writing his "Autobiographical Notes."

1886

Joins the culture and arts club Ateneu Barcelonès. Maragall's father announces to the family that a poor investment in industrial hemp has cost him half his fortune. Maragall takes over and puts the family economy back on track. Completes his "Autobiographical Notes" at age twenty-five, writing: "Here ends my youth. A work of genius, *Werther*, took me from boyhood to adolescence. An event, the loss of half the family fortune, has taken me from adolescence to manhood. Life's most happy age, good-bye forever! Dreams of love and glory, farewell!" In Puigcerdà, during summer, introduced by a friend from university to Teresa Ferran, whom he agrees to call on, though he confides to Lloret that he still prefers Amanda. Meets Francesc Matheu, editor of *La Ilustració Catalana*, the first magazine of art, literature and science in Catalan.

1887

Teresa Ferran's mother accepts Maragall, who initiates a courtship with her daughter; perceiving, however, insufficient enthusiasm in Maragall, the mother breaks off the relationship. Maragall undergoes an emotional crisis.

1888

Publishes "L'oda infinita" ("Endless Ode") in *La Ilustració Catalana*. Crisis continues until summer, in Puigcerdà, where Maragall meets Clara Noble Malvido (1872-1944), his future wife, who was then sixteen years old. Resigns himself to being a run-of-the-mill lawyer of modest ambition.

1890

Begins working in the law offices of Josep Víctor Brugada, in com-
bination with his own clients. Initiates written correspondence with
Clara Noble. Begins working at the daily newspaper *Diario de Barcelona* as contributor and secretary to editor-in-chief Joan Mañé i
Flaquer. Continues working as a lawyer.

1891

Courtship with Clara Noble. Maragall spends part of the summer
with Clara and her family at Las Arenas beach, Getxo (province of
Biscay, Basque Country). Wedding at Santa Anna Church, Barce-
lona, on 27 December. Maragall's friends present him with a limited
edition of *Poesías: originals y traduccions* (Barcelona: La Ilustracío
Catalana, 1891) containing fourteen of his poems and five of his
Catalan translations of poems by Goethe. Honeymoon trip to Nice,
Montecarlo, Florence, Pisa, Genova, and Marseille.

1892

The newly wedded couple moves into an apartment at number 2,
1, 2, Carrer Roger de Llúria. Maragall publishes his first extensive
opinion article, "El Paraguay," in the *Diario de Barcelona*. Between
1892 and 1903 he would publish 248 articles.

1893

Discovers Nietzsche. Birth of Maragall's first daughter, Helena.
Publishes his first article in Catalan: "Nietzsche." Summer sojourn at
Sant Joan de les Abadesses, where he composes "La vaca cega" ("The
Cow Gone Blind"). Attempted assassination of Spanish military offi-
cer Arsenio Martínez Campos, Captain-General of Catalonia, on
24 September. Bomb attack in the Liceu on 7 November during a

performance attended by Maragall, prompting the composition of the poem "Paternal" ("Fatherhood").

1894

Awarded prize at Barcelona's Jocs Florals for the poem "La sardana." Birth of second daughter, Maria.

1895

The Maragall family moves into a new apartment at number 64, 2, Passeig de Gràcia. Publishes *Poesies*. Death of Willie Noble, Maragall's brother-in-law, prompting composition of "En la mort d'un jove" ("At a Young Man's Death"). Participates in the capacity of general secretary of the Ateneu Barcelonès in the proceedings of the opening of the academic year, presided by Àngel Guimerà, who delivered the ceremonial speech in Catalan for the first time in the history of the institution.

1896

Awarded prize at Barcelona's Jocs Florals for the poem "El mal caçador" ("The Impious Hunter"). The Maragall family moves to an apartment at number 344, 3, 2, Carrer Consell de Cent. Birth of third daughter, Eulàlia.

1897

Meets Andalusian philosopher and educator Francisco Giner de los Ríos in Barcelona.

1898

Composes "Oda a Espanya" ("Ode to Spain"), motivated by the disastrous denouement of Spanish colonialism. Enric Prat de la

Riba offers Maragall the job of editor-in-chief of the soon-to-be-relaunched daily *La Veu de Catalunya*, which Maragall declines.

1899

Birth of fourth and fifth daughters (twins) Clara and Anna. The Maragall family moves to number 79, Carrer Alfons XII, in the Sant Gervasi district (Maragall's final Barcelona residence, today the site of the Joan Maragall Archive).

1900

Death of Maragall's father. Birth of sixth child (the first boy), Josep. Publishes *Visions & Cants* (Visions & Songs). Visits Madrid and Toledo.

1901

Diagnosed with what was then called neurasthenia, exhibited fatigue and anxiety; given sick leave by a medical board. Maragall moves to Vilafranca del Penedès where he works briefly as land registrar for friend Antoni Roura, assigned to the Philippines in 1889 and with whom Maragall maintained frequent correspondence. Return to Barcelona. First family sojourn in Caldetes (Caldes d'Estrach). Composes "Vistes al mar" ("Views of the Sea"). Death of Joan Mañé i Flaquer. Summer sojourn in Camprodon; travels to Toulouse, Cauterets, Lourdes, Gavarnie, Pau, Carcassonne, Elna and Olot. Return to Barcelona. Recommences publishing articles for the *Diario de Barcelona*, now on a weekly basis.

1902

Travels again to Cauterets, Lourdes and Pau. Return to Barcelona. Birth of seventh child (second boy), Joan Anton. Maragall publishes the article "La patria nueva" ("The New Country"), for which charges are brought against him.

1903

Death of Maragall's mother. Leaves the *Diario de Barcelona*. Sits on the judges' panel of Barcelona's Jocs Florals. Appointed president of the Ateneu Barcelonès. Travels to San Sebastián, Bilbao and A Coruña. Return to Barcelona. Delivers the inaugural address at the Ateneu Barcelonès: "Elogi de la paraula" ("In Praise of Words"). Birth of eighth child, Ernest. Maragall's play *La Margarideta* (scenes from Faust translated by Maragall) premieres at the Teatre de les Arts, directed by Adrià Gual; poor critical reception because of "Catalanizing" the scenes. Publishes the first serial appearance of poems from *Les disperses* (Scatterings) in the weekly magazine *Joventut*.

1904

Begins publishing articles in *La Ilustració Catalana* on a regular basis, writing twenty-two articles from 1904 to 1906. Awarded prize at Barcelona's Jocs Florals for the poem "Glosa" (Ballad). Completion of term as president of the Ateneu Barcelonès (succeeded by Lluís Domènech i Montaner). Summer sojourn with family in Blanes. Travels alone to Cauterets, via Toulouse, where he finishes composing the second part of *El comte Arnau* and rereads *Don Quijote*. Returns to Blanes and makes final revisions of *Artículos*, published this same year. Return to Barcelona.

1905

Visits Poblet with friends Antoni Roura and Josep Pijoan, historian and writer Antoni Rubió i Lluch, and prominent Catalan statesman Francesc Cambó. Travels to Cauterets via Toulouse, Pau and Lourdes. Return to Barcelona. Begins writing again for the *Diario de Barcelona* under its new editor-in-chief Miquel dels S. Oliver. Birth of ninth child, Guillem. Maragall travels to Olot, where he receives an invitation by messenger to stand for election with the Lliga Regionalista, the influential conservative pro-Catalan party under the leadership of Francesc Cambó, Enric Prat de la Riba and others; Maragall declines. Return to Barcelona. Sojourn in Girona to preside the city's Jocs Florals ceremony.

1906

Pays a visit to Bishop Josep Torras i Bages with architect Antoni Gaudí and friend Josep Pijoan. Publishes *Enllà* (Beyond). Again leaves the *Diario de Barcelona* along with the editor-in-chief and other pro-Catalan contributors. Sojourn in Blanes; reads Virgil, Ramon Muntaner, and translates Novalis. Return to Barcelona. Travels to Cauterets with his sisters via Toulouse, then to Lourdes and Pau. Reads Anatole France. Joins family in Blanes. Return to Barcelona and birth of tenth child, Ramon. Participates in the First International Conference on the Catalan Language. Completes translation of Novalis's *Heinrich von Ofterdingen*, published the following year.

1907

First visit to Lleida, where Maragall presides the city's Jocs Florals. Sojourns in Caldetes and Olot. Writes abundant prose: "Elogi de la poesia," "De la poesía" and "Elogi del poble;" in all, sixteen articles appearing in *La Lectura* and later published in the posthumous volume *Elogios*. Birth of eleventh child, Elvira.

1908

Summer sojourn in Caldetes and Olot. Begins writing *Nausica* (Nausicaa).

1909

Birth of twelfth child, Gabriel. Bishop Torras i Bages confirms seven of Maragall's children. Setmana Tràgica (Tragic Week) of 26-31 July occurs while Maragall is in Caldetes. Returns briefly to Barcelona, then back to Caldetes, Olot, and finally Barcelona again. Publishes "Ah! Barcelona…" in *La Veu de Catalunya* on 1 October. Sends his second Tragic Week article, "La ciutat del perdó" ("City of Pardon") to *La Veu de Catalunya*, only to be rejected by editor-in-chief Enric Prat de la Riba. Publishes his third Tragic Week article, "L'església cremada" ("The Church After Burning") in *La Veu de Catalunya* on 18 December.

1910

Completes the composition of "Cant espiritual" ("Spiritual") on 4 February. Death of friend Antoni Roura on 19 February. Summer sojourn in Caldetes; continues writing and completes *Nausica*. Return to Barcelona. Writes a second "Autobiographical Notes" at age fifty. Writes the essays "Del vivir" and "De la gracia."

1911

Birth of thirteenth (and last) child, Jordi. Publishes *Seqüències* (Sequences). In February appointed member of the future Philological Section of the Institut d'Estudis Catalans, to be inaugurated in May. Completes his biography of Joan Mañé i Flaquer. Paid a visit by members of the Cercle Conservador, who invite him to write again in the *Diario de Barcelona* in view of plans to make changes in the newspaper; Maragall agrees, but does not write political articles. Sojourns in Caldetes after visiting Cauterets, Toulouse and Pau. Return to Caldetes. Travels to Castellterçol with his two eldest daughters, then returns to Caldetes. Return to Barcelona. Maragall's son Gabriel, in his account of 30 November, later writes that: "After playing two Beethoven sonatas on the piano and winding the clock in the dining room, he went to his bedroom before the accustomed hour." The following day he did not get up. Death of Maragall on 20 December. Medical reports indicate fevers as the cause of death.

ONE DAY OF LIFE
IS LIFE

FROM POEMS
(*POESIES*, 1895)

On the occasion of his wedding to Clara Noble Malvido (1872-1944) on 27 December 1891, Maragall was presented with a limited edition (101 copies) containing fourteen of his poems and five of his Catalan translations of poems by Johann Wolfgang von Goethe. This chapbook was prepared by thirteen of his friends, including literary critics Joan Sardà i Lloret (1851-1898), Josep Soler i Miquel (1861-1897), Josep Yxart i de Moragas (1852-1895); writer and publisher Francesc Matheu i Fornells (1851-1938); and renowned novelist Narcís Oller i Moragas (1846-1930). The 104-page volume, titled *Poesías: originals y traduccions* (Barcelona: La Ilustració Catalana, 1891), laid the groundwork for the first book of poems—revised, restructured and expanded—to be published by Maragall four years later: *Poesies* (Barcelona: L'Avenç, 1895). The gift was, as Joan-Lluís Marfany and Glòria Casals point out, a landmark moment: beaconing Maragall's recognition by literary peers as a poet of talent (see Marfany 1986, 191; Casals 1998, 75). Readers of poetry being few, however, Maragall would long remain more widely known for his engaging opinion articles featured in the conservative-leaning Spanish-language daily *Diario de Barcelona* (see Pijoan 2010, 48), which from 1892 to 1903 published two hundred forty-eight articles penned by Maragall (see Moreta 2010, 474).

In *Poesies,* five of the original fourteen poems in the chapbook published by his friends were now reorganized into the single series poem "Festeig vora la mar cantàbrica" ("Courtship by the Bay of Biscay") and three others also reappeared, slightly revised, including the prologue poem "L'oda infinita" ("Endless Ode"). After the prologue poem come four more sections: *Claror* (Clarity) with eight poems; *Pirinenques* (Pyrenean Poems), a suite of six poems followed by two more; *Tríptic de l'any* (Seasons Triptych), three poems; and the epilogue poem "Excèlsior" ("Excelsior"). D. Sam Abrams has identified the book's underlying theme as "the indissoluble bond between poetry and life," where *Claror* poeticizes "human relationships, represented by love and family," *Pirinenques* evokes our "links with nature, evinced in [the poet's] visits to the Pyrenees;" finally, *Tríptic de l'any* shows our "spiritual relations with the transcendent by means of celebrations of importance throughout the Christological year" (2010, 20).

Although Maragall's poems had appeared in various Barcelona publications as early as 1878, it is widely agreed that Maragall's outstanding works "begin with 'L'oda infinita,' which draws a clear dividing line between his poetic prehistory and history" (Marfany 1986, 193). First published on 30 April 1888 in the literary magazine *La Ilustració Catalana* (see Moreta 2010, 468), the poem is an affirmation of Maragall's conviction that poetry is for him a vocation, a calling which "he cannot elude" and that has become both the "driving force and aim" of his life, and the two are inextricably interwoven: "Poetry is not produced, it is living. As a result, the poet does not write poems, concrete artefacts that turn into separate things once written—the poet enacts or carries out a work, the very ode that will end only with the poet's death" (Marfany 1986, 194).

The next three poems in our selection are taken from *Claror*. In her inquiry into the role of the women who made an impact on Maragall and his poetry throughout his life, Casals points out the lexico-semantic affinity between his wife's given name, Clara, and the Catalan word *claror* (the effect of light that makes things visible), adding powerful connotative value to the epithet heading the section that spotlights the poet's courtship, nuptials, wedding trip and parenthood in tandem with Clara Noble (see Casals 2011a, 40). It has been said that this suite, poeticizing the early highlights of Maragall's loving relationship with Clara Noble, "has always been seen as the definitive manifestation of Maragall's poetic maturity," a "sudden blooming" brought forth by his love for Clara; Maragall himself "would say that he had done all in life late, and that among other things, he had not felt the 'full sensation of youth' until age thirty-one" (Marfany 1986, 195-196).

Some, if not all, of "Festeig vora la mar cantàbrica" was composed by Maragall during his summer sojourn at Las Arenas Beach, north of Bilbao, where he joined the Noble–Malvido family after the announcement of his engagement to Clara in May 1891; Maragall sent part of the poem to his friend Josep Soler i Miquel in a letter dated 17 August (see Casals 1998, 111; Moreta 2010, 473). Abrams has pointed out the poem's unequivocally modern character: "the fragmented poetic discourse embodies or represents an unconstant state of consciousness and a perception of partial or intermittent reality," a technique that would become "one of the most frequent mechanisms of modern poetry from the 1920s onward" (2010, 34).

In "Nuvial" ("Wedded") Maragall depicts and reflects on his wedding, the wedding trip through Provence and into Italy, the sojourns in Genoa and Florence, and the return to Barcelona. Originally published in *La Ilustració Catalana* (31 July 1892) under the title "Resposta" (Reply), the poem was Maragall's response to the verse dedication— written by Sardà on behalf of the poet's friends— that appeared on the opening pages of the wedding-gift chapbook (this verse dedication was also published in *La Ilustració Catalana*, 15 January 1892) (see Casals 1998, 123). The emotive impact of the poem is subtle yet powerful, striking a remarkable balance between the wonder and self-discovery in the poet's newfound matrimonial love and his deep-felt brotherly and collegial love for his close literary friends:

"Don't get the idea," writes Maragall to Soler i Miquel, "that conjugal love is so very all-absorbing: on the contrary, it summons all other affections." Indeed, the Maragall–Noble marriage was capable of combining family and friendships, as shown by Maragall's receiving his friends at home, the closest of whom were now also family friends. (Moreta 2010, 100)

The resulting balance is one that is respectfully but vitally inclusive: "But don't let's box love in: it should expand and spread, / so those around me who've been true / might, around you, come into view. / Not love only courses through my veins: / other concerns have captained my life, / and your gaze grows softer in my eyes / when I open them up to a measureless clarity." Here we sense the strong connection between the smaller circles of intimate love and the wider-rippling public-spirited love that will emerge powerfully in Maragall's later writings, especially in the wake of the Tragic Week of 1909 (see, in this selection, the articles "Ah! Barcelona…," "City of Pardon," and "The Church After Burning;" and the extraordinary poem "New Ode to Barcelona").

The hard-hitting short poem "Paternal" ("Fatherhood") was

written after a small but deadly bomb was tossed into the orchestra seats in Barcelona's Liceu Opera House, killing twenty people, during the performance of Gioacchino Rossini's *William Tell* on 7 November 1893. The bomber, Santiago Salvador, was driven by the execution, a month earlier, of anarchist Paulí Pallàs, who had attempted to assassinate the Captain General of Catalonia, Arsenio Martínez Campos. Maragall attended the performance that evening, accompanied by his wife, parents and sisters; he composed the poem that same evening at home (see Casals 1998, 134). Abrams, in his close examination of the poem's versification, shows how Maragall breaks stanzaic conventions using a Castilian-style five-line lira stanza in lines 5 through 9, and his third stanza metrifies inversely the pattern of the first stanza (2010, 60-61). This break with formal convention is part and parcel of the poem's clash with thematic convention, accounting for its mixed reception in the Catalan literary canon over the years (53-54):

It could not be a "normal" poem, a traditional poem with all its elements regulated and under control. It had to be broken up, irregular, problematic.

[…] Maragall knew that the new content required a new formulation of poetic discourse […] the content could not be forced into the straitjacket of established tradition, and the irregular and innovative form sought to imitate the atmosphere in the opera house—unprecedented, out-of-control. (62)

"All in all," writes Abrams, "with 'Paternal' the poet tossed a bomb into the orchestra seats of Catalan poetry" (58). Separately, or perhaps tangentially, Maragall's enthusiasm for Nietzschean vitalism at the time he wrote this poem is, as has often been pointed out, a key element here, as is the connection between the "innocent child" in the poem and that of *Also sprach Zarathustra*, fragments of which

Maragall had been translating (see Abrams, 56-59; Casals 1998, 134-135). The child's "barbaric laugh" at the poem's end suggests the thin line between regeneration and destruction.

"La vaca cega" ("The Cow Gone Blind") is the second of the three poems in the *Pirinenques* section of *Poesies*. Written in the summer of 1893 during a family sojourn in the town of Sant Joan de les Abadesses in the Pyrenees, it has been called "one of the best known and least understood" of Maragall's poems (Abrams 2010, 71), and illustrates perfectly how he "always worked with the noble raw material provided for him by immediate reality" (71). Forty-two years after the event that gave rise to the poem, Maragall's widow Clara Noble would write:

We spent the days at a cousin's house and in the afternoons, together with Maragall's parents, who were getting on in years, and my sisters and the children and the nannies, we would all go to the spring by the name of Covilar just outside the town on the road to Camprodon. The spring flowed into a trough in a little square with trees and benches. One day we were startled by a cow moving towards us—she walked apprehensively, hesitatingly, strangely. I can picture her now. Everyone got up and left except for my husband. He stayed put. It was the cow gone blind! As she drank, Maragall spoke with the boy whose "aim [was] a little too good" and had put out one of her eyes. When he got home he went straight to his study, shut the door, and when he came out he had the poem in his hand. A few days later he sent that copy to his good friend Soler i Miquel. (quoted in Abrams 2010, 72)

Arguing against a conservative, sentimental strain of critical canon, Abrams contends that the strength of this poem lies precisely in the unsettling and irreconcilable sensation that it produces in the reader, which is a mirror of that same disturbing and irreconcilable sensation caused in the poet by the appearance of the animal:

[Maragall] confronts us with reality, he makes us see it in all its beauty and ugliness, harmony and disorder, peace and violence. As in "Paternal," he is unwilling to speak only about the bright and ordered side of life. Life is a whole and one cannot turn away from anything that makes up a part of reality. (75)

Consistent with Maragall's theoretical construct of the "living word," the poet uses language to translate sensations directly into poetry, which mirrors them or relays them unfiltered—as far as this is possible—to the reader. Maragall's moving poetic account of the animal's visit to the spring is disarmingly objective in tone, punctuated, it has been noted, only by the emotive elements "a gesture that is grand and tragic" and "unforgettable," which "break with the apparently impersonal" tone of the description (Marfany 1986, 198). All in all, we are struck by "the sincerity of [Maragall's] compassion: a restrained compassion which corresponds in a way to the resignation of the animal itself" (Terry 2001, 9).

Closing the volume, the epilogue poem "Excèlsior" ("Excelsior") points the way toward the future of the man and the poet, where poetry and life are hardwired into one. While the opening poem "L'oda infinita" underscored the vitalism driving the poet, "Excèlsior" poeticizes the vitalism driving the man, ever forward, ever outward: "Away land and beach behind, / oblivious to all returning: / there is no end in sight, / there's to be no end to your journey." The precise date of composition is unknown, but the poem's title appears with exclamatory force in an article of Maragall's titled—oxymoronically—"La juventud conservadora" (Conservative Youth), published in *Diario de Barcelona* on 3 December 1892; accordingly, Casals dates the poem generally between 1892 and 1894 (1998, 193). In any event, "Excèlsior" is certainly a "critical reply" (Abrams 2010, 117) to the poem "Joventut" (Youth, 1885) by Mallorcan poet-priest Miquel Costa i Llobera (1844-1922). Maragall was surely acquainted also with the Henry Wadsworth Longfellow (1807-1882) poem "Excelsior," included in Spanish translation in *Poesías de los principales autores modernos* (València: Pascual Aguilar, 1875[?]) by renowned Valencian poet and journalist Teodor Llorente i Olivares (1836-1911), a copy of which Maragall had in his library (see Casals 1998, 192). Separately, Catalan composer Felip Pedrell (1841-1922) converted the Longfellow poem into his symphonic poem *Excelsior* (1880); and it was Pedrell who would later compose the opera *El comte Arnau* (1904) based on the first part of Maragall's poem of the same name (see headnote to *Visions & Cants*).

L'ODA INFINITA

Tinc una oda començada
que no puc acabar mai;
dia i nit me l'ha dictada
tot quant canta en la ventada,
5   tot quant brilla per l'espai.

Va entonar-la ma infantesa
entre ensomnis d'amor pur;
decaiguda i mig malmesa,
joventut me l'ha represa
10   amb compàs molt més segur.

De seguida, amb veu més forta
m'han sigut dictats nous cants;
pro, cada any que el temps s'emporta,
veig una altra esparsa morta
15   i perduts els consonants.

Ja no sé com començava
ni sé com acabarà,
perquè tinc la pensa esclava
d'una força que s'esbrava
20   dictant-me-la sens parar.

I aixís sempre, a la ventura,
sens saber si lliga o no,
va enllaçant la mà insegura
crits de goig, planys d'amargura,
25   himnes d'alta adoració.

ENDLESS ODE

There's an ode that I've begun
and never can complete,
dictated to me night and day
by all that sings on the breeze,
5   by all that shimmers in space.

It sang out from my childhood
in dreams of purest love,
but seeing how it lacked revision,
my later youth would take it up
10   and give it gauge and rhythm.

Soon, in a voice still stronger,
there came to me new songs;
yet with each year time takes away
I find another stanza's gone
15   and consonants are swept away.

I don't know how it started
or how it is to end,
I only know my mind's held siege:
captive to a force that's spent
20   dictating to me ceaselessly.

And so it happens that by chance,
not knowing if they match,
my own uncertain hand entwines
now cries of joy, now sorrow's pangs,
25   now hymns of piety sublime.

Sols desitjo, per ma glòria,
que si algú aquesta oda sap,
al moment en què jo mòria,
me la diga de memòria
30 mot per mot, de cap a cap.

Me la diga a cau d'orella
esbrinant-me, fil per fil,
de la ignota meravella
que a la vida ens aparella
35 el teixit ferm i subtil.

I sabré si en lo que penses
—oh poeta extasiat!—
hi ha un ressò de les cadences
de l'aucell d'ales immenses
40 que nia en l'eternitat.

My only wish, my one delight,
is that whoever might know
this ode the moment of my death,
let them recite it to me whole:
30   word for word from start to end.

Let them whisper it to my ear,
unraveling, thread by thread,
the well-knit, subtle fabric of
that undiscovered wonder whence
35   life is bound and linked with us.

And I'll know if in your thoughts
there are measures to be heard
—O poet in your ecstasy!—
echoing from the great-winged bird
40   that nests in all eternity.

FESTEIG VORA LA MAR CANTÀBRICA

I

Per lla a la migdiada resplendenta,
des de la platja a la llunyana bruma,
canta i s'adorm al sol la mar brunzenta,
descabdellant i cabdellant escuma.

II

5 Mira avançar-se cap a tu les ones
formant graons festonejats d'escuma:
la immensa escala va acostant-se ràpida
temptadora als teus peus. Oh, no! No fugis:
els graons menyspreuats se desvaneixen
10 per l'oblidat sorral; pro, quants ne vénen
de l'inflamat ponent, interminables!

Seguim la llum per sobre el mar. Que onades
hi deuríem trobar endintre, endintre!
Les que eixa nit han d'arribar a la platja,
15 les de demà, i encar les d'altres dies,
les que encara són lluny i que s'afanyen
caminant cap aquí, les sents que vénen?
....
La nit s'estén per tot, la mar ressona.

III

Sota les estrelles, d'espatlles al mar,
20 una galta humida, fresca de serena,

COURTSHIP BY THE BAY OF BISCAY

I

Stretched beneath the brilliant noon
from beach to sea-mists far away,
whitecaps wobbling in the sun,
there drones the songful, sleepy bay.

II

5   See the waves draw close to you,
laying stairs festooned with foam:
the rolling staircase rushes in
tempting at your feet. No! Don't run:
the misprized stairs soon vanish
10 in sands forgotten; but look how many
roll unending from the burning west!

Let's follow the light over the sea: what waves
we'd find, farther and farther out!
Those to reach the shore tonight,
15 those of tomorrow, and days to come,
and those, far-off still, yet eager:
can you hear them now on their way?

....

The night spreads all round, the sea resounds.

III

Beneath the stars, our backs to the bay,
20 a moist cheek, cool from the night air,

una galta suau i plena
és ben dolça de besar.
Entre dos silencis, bes silenciós,
com vares deixar-nos tremolant tots dos
25 dins la nit quieta amb deixos ardents
de la migdiada i dels terrals vents.

El reberes silenciosa.
Mos llavis, dolços encar,
te van preguntar una cosa,
30 i tu no em vas contestar.
Què vaig preguntar-te?… Sols recordo el bes
i que sentia la plena mar alta.
Tu, tota caiguda, semblaves malalta…
Oh! No hi tornaré mai més.

35 Pro la flonja galta ruixada amb serena,
sota de ma boca, d'espatlles al mar;
pro la xafogosa nit d'agost serena
ai! com la podré oblidar?

IV

Quin rebolcar-se avui totes les ones
40 escumejant sorroses, desiguals!
Com s'estiren i s'alcen tant com poden
per a fugir el gran turment del mar!

Tot el mar s'ensombreix i se sorolla,
ones vénen arreu, onades van,
45 corrent cap a la platja clamoroses,
l'escabellada escuma al vent donant.

a cheek soft and full
brings joy to kiss.
Between two silences, silent kiss,
how you left the two of us trembling
25   in the standstill night with sweltry traces
of the noon and land-warm winds.

Silently you received it.
Still soft, my lips
asked you something,
30   but you gave no answer.
What did I ask you?… I remember only the kiss
and hearing the open sea.
You, suddenly languid, seemed ill…
I'll never go back there again.

35   But your soft, soft cheek sprayed with starlight,
beneath my lips, our backs to the sea,
and the sultry August night, its stillness:
how could I forget?

IV

What turmoil the waves raise today
40   furious and foaming with sand!
How they rear and reach high as they can
and flee the woes of the troubled bay!

The great seascape darkens and groans,
waves hunching and pitching everywhere,
45   clamoring onward to the shore,
tossing their ruffled foam on the wind.

V

Adéu

Per què avui ets tan hermosa,
tan blavosa i aplanada,
mar cantàbrica febrosa
50   tan sovint, tan agitada?
Tu, que saps llançar al cel
tanta escuma lluminosa
en els jorns de tes grans ires;
tu, que avances i et retires,
55   governant pluges i vents,
amorosa avui t'estens;
en tos llavis la lleugera
i blanquíssima bromera,
en tos llavis l'himne suau,
60   el teu llom ratllat d'esteles,
damunt teu, sota el cel blau,
blanc eixam d'alegres veles…
Bé recordo ta inquietud
quan un dia i altre dia
65   en ton llit te removia
un turment desconegut.
Jo he escoltat ton etern «ai!»
solitari de la nit,
aquell enrogallat crit
70   que no s'acabava mai.
I t'he vist brau i joiós
de ta escuma que enlluerna,
esborronat i negrós

V

Good-bye

How is it that today you're so lovely,
so blue and smooth-lying,
Cantabrian Sea so feverish
50 at times, so turbulent?
You, who hurl to the sky
so much gleaming froth
on days you're seized with rage;
you, who approach, then draw back,
55 governing winds and rains,
today you lie lovingly;
on your lips the sparkle
of splashing surf,
and a soft anthem,
60 your back grooved with furrows;
above you, beneath a blue sky,
a shimmering swarm of bright sails…
I still recall your restlessness
on this or that day when
65 some uncharted storm set you
tossing and turning in your bed.
I've heard your timeless wail
alone in the night,
the throaty cry
70 that knew no end.
I've seen you fine and cheerful
in your shining surf,
dark and disturbed

sota el cop de la galerna,
75 inflat d'immensos sospirs
d'un fatic que mai no para,
verd i blanc com prat amb llirs…
Pro mai tan hermós com ara.

when struck by north-west gales,
75   swelling with enormous sighs
beneath no end of burdens,
green and white like pastures strewn with lilies…
But never so beautiful as now.

NUVIAL

Resplendenta, sencera, arrodonida,
s'alça per sobre el mar la lluna plena:
així sento pujar la meva vida,
astre sense minvant en nit serena.

5   Dels braços dels amics als de l'aimada,
un moment vaig sentir l'esgarrifosa
gran buidor de l'espai…
                 Sota l'arcada
del temple, ressonanta i tenebrosa,
davant del nostre *sí* l'altar floria,

10   revestint-se de llum i d'alegria.
Però una gran tristor, a l'esposa honesta,
a l'espòs pensatiu, els inundava,
que darrera d'aquell altar en festa
quelcom cantant fugia i s'allunyava.

15   Jo me la vaig endur, en la nit confosa,
de l'enclòs maternal, com presonera,
i ella girava el cap tota plorosa,
fins a ser-ne ben lluny, sempre endarrera.
Anàrem per la nit. Fou agonia

20   d'una vida, i d'una altra fou naixença…
Després se'ns va aclarir vermell el dia
per les severes planes de Provença.
Llavors, la vida nova ben resolta,
de fit a fit els ulls, les testes altes,

25   ens vam mirar per la primera volta…

WEDDED

Resplendent, complete, round as can be,
the full moon lifts above the sea:
that's how I feel my life rising,
unwaning orb in the crystalline night.

5 From the arms of friends to the arms I love,
I felt, for a shuddering moment,
the huge emptiness of space…
                    Beneath the arching
temple, with its echoes and its shadows,
at our *Yes* the altar broke into bloom,

10 radiant with light and cheer.
But then a gloom came over
the true-hearted bride, the pensive groom,
as behind that festive altar, a something
in song moved off, took flight.

15 I led her, in the vague night,
from her mother's hearth as if a captive,
and she turned her head to look behind,
tears in her eyes, till far away.
We walked in the night. These were the death-throes

20 of a life, and birth of another…
Afterwards, the day sparkled red
over the harsh plains of Provence.
Then, our new life all arranged,
we looked each other, heads high,

25 straight in the eye for the first time—

i no hi hagué vergonya en nostres galtes.
—I, ara, vers sol ixent. La Itàlia ens rebi
hostes devots —vam dir. I, de passada,
inquiets travessàrem l'hivern tebi,
30 sobredaurat, de Niça aviciada.
Un moment va cobrir Gènova airosa
amb son llampant mantell nostres delícies;
rebérem de la plana marismosa
de Pisa melancòliques carícies;
35 mes com acer a qui l'imant demana
i sent, com més a prop, més influència,
creuàrem per la plàcida Toscana
emportats pel teu màgic nom... Florència!
A Florència ja som. Desperta, aimada!
40 Contemplem, en Florència, la florida
que treu el món quan l'hora és arribada
de les grans primaveres de la vida:
mira la gran iglésia assoleiada
amb la volta amplament arrodonida;
45 mira marbres florir de tota espècie,
i mira en els altars el Déu de Grècia.
¿No veus l'Apol·lo aquí d'un antic temple
en la forma d'eix sant, blanca i serena,
i com en els seus peus avui contempla,
50 mig rient, aquest culte d'altra mena?
Veu flors i marbre blanc; sent a tothora
perfums en l'aire i notes d'harmonia;
i té la llum del sol que l'acolora,
virolats raigs que el finestral destria.
55 La catedral, al sol estarrufada,

and there wasn't any shame in our cheeks.
"And now, to the east! Let Italy greet
her earnest guests," said we. And making our way,
we crossed, restless, the tepid gilded
30   wintertime of pampered Nice.
For a moment graceful Genoa draped
our delights beneath her bright blanket;
and from the marshy stretches of Pisa
we gathered melancholy caresses;
35   but as steel summoned by a magnet,
feeling its pull augment as we approached,
we passed over placid Tuscony
drawn by your magical name—Florence!
And so finally, Florence. Wake up, my love!
40   See how in Florence the world
gives bloom when the hour strikes
the magnificent springtimes of life:
see the great church drenched in sunshine,
how its wide rounded vault rises;
45   see every species of marble in flower,
and see on her altars the gods of Greece.
Can you see some ancient temple's Apollo
now here as this saint, white and serene;
and how at his feet he surveys today,
50   half-smiling, this sect of another stamp?
He takes in flowers and niveous marble,
and airborne perfumes and tunes at all hours,
and sunshine to keep him warm,
in beams tall windows deploy into color.
55   The cathedral, swelling in the sun,

triomfadora en colors clars s'ostenta,
i allà en la *Sacrestia* retirada
la immensa *Notte* blanca jau potenta.

Mes quan la negra nit pausada arriba,
60 damunt les florentines meravelles
s'aixeca una figura pensativa
que porta el front tot coronat d'estrelles.
Gibel·lí per qui l'Arno encar murmura
tornaveus d'una lluita sens clemència,
65 viatger estrany de l'encontrada obscura...
És el trist Dante que ensombreix Florència.

....

Anem's-en ja d'aquí, que jo m'enyoro:
a la terra tornem dels amors nostres,
on jo retrobi, amb l'alè usat que adoro,
70 l'inoblidat caient dels amics rostres;
perquè l'escalf de l'última encaixada
ha covat en ma sang com una pira,
que avui s'alça brillant i incendiada,
i el vent d'amor cap a ponent la tira.

75 Allí la casa nuvial espera
a l'espòs que captiva hi duu l'esposa.
Captiva sols d'amor... reina que impera,
al posar-hi les mans, en cada cosa;
i reina del sentit de l'home encara.

80 Mes no encongim l'amor: campi i rumbegi,
i a quants m'han estimat ara i ans d'ara
al meu entorn, al teu entorn els vegi.
No sols d'amor m'han bategat mos polsos:
altres afanys han governat ma vida,

glows triumphant in pale hues;
and there in the *Sagrestia* reclines,
great and white, *Notte* in all her power.
But when nightfall, dark and still, descends
60 on all these Florentine marvels,
a pensive figure rises up:
seen to be wearing a crown of stars.
Ghibelline for whom the Arno's endless
murmur echoes war inclement,
65 strange traveler in a land uncertain…
Sad Dante spreads gloom over Florence.

             ……………………………………………

Let's go back then, I miss home:
back again, to the land of our loves,
and meet again, in the relished speech,
70 the indelible etchings of friends' faces;
because the warmth of those last handshakes
now rekindle in my blood like a pyre,
today a brilliant blaze
that winds of love would now speed westward.
75 There, the nuptial home awaits
the groom who brings the bride now captive.
Captive—only of love: queen sovereign
at a hand's touch of all things;
and queen, still, of the meaning of man.
80 But don't let's box love in: it should expand and spread,
so those around me who've been true
might, around you, come into view.
Not love only courses through my veins:
other concerns have captained my life,

85 i em seran tos esguards als ulls més dolços
si els tinc oberts a una claror sens mida…
Mes, en tant, tu descansa, refiada,
sobre els genolls del teu marit, que espia
en el tomb de ta cara esbarrellada
90 la inquietud de l'infant que s'anuncia.

85 and your gaze grows softer in my eyes
when I open them up to a measureless clarity...
Meanwhile, rest yourself, heart at ease,
here on the knees of your husband, who catches sight
in the features of your paling face
90 of the restlessness of the child on its way.

PATERNAL

TORNANT DEL LICEU EN LA NIT DEL

7 DE NOVEMBRE DE 1893.

Furient va esclatant l'odi per la terra,
regalen sang les coll-torçades testes,
    i cal anar a les festes
amb pit ben esforçat, com a la guerra.

5 A cada esclat mortal — la gent trèmola es gira:
la crueltat que avança, — la por que s'enretira,
    se van partint el món…
Mirant al fill que mama, — a la mare que sospira,
    el pare arruga el front.

10   Pro l'infant innocent,
que deixa, satisfet, la buidada mamella,
    se mira an ell, — se mira an ella,
    i riu bàrbarament.

FATHERHOOD

ON COMING HOME FROM THE LICEU OPERA HOUSE
THE NIGHT OF 7 NOVEMBER 1893.

Furious, hate breaks out on the earth,
from heads on twisted necks blood pours,
    and nerves of steel are advised
when off to soirées or to war.

5 With each fatal attack — we turn and shudder:
cruelty advances — fear moves back:
    dividing the world between them…
Eyeing the suckling child — and sighing mother,
    the father knits a brow.

10   But the innocent child,
now sated, releases the drained breast,
    gazes at him — then at her,
    and lets go a barbaric laugh.

LA VACA CEGA

Topant de cap en una i altra soca,
avançant d'esma pel camí de l'aigua,
se'n ve la vaca tota sola. És cega.
D'un cop de roc llançat amb massa traça,
5   el vailet va buidar-li un ull, i en l'altre
se li ha posat un tel. La vaca és cega.
Ve a abeurar-se a la font com ans solia;
mes no amb el ferm posat d'altres vegades
ni amb ses companyes, no: ve tota sola.
10   Ses companyes, pels cingles, per les comes,
pel silenci dels prats i en la ribera,
fan dringar l'esquellot mentres pasturen
l'herba fresca a l'atzar... Ella cauria.
Topa de morro en l'esmolada pica
15   i recula afrontada... Però torna
i abaixa el cap a l'aigua i beu calmosa.
Beu poc, sens gaire set... Després aixeca
al cel, enorme, l'embanyada testa
amb un gran gesto tràgic; parpelleja
20   damunt les mortes nines, i se'n torna
orfa de llum, sota del sol que crema,
vacil·lant pels camins inoblidables,
brandant lànguidament la llarga cua.

THE COW GONE BLIND

Her head bumping on one trunk after another,
stepping by rote along the water path,
a cow approaches all alone. She's blind.
A rock once thrown by a boy, his aim a little
5   too good, put out an eye, and a gluey film
has claimed her sight in the other. The cow is blind.
She comes to drink just like before at the spring;
but not so self-assured as other times
nor with others of her kind: she's all alone.
10   Her sisters, wandering over summits and hollows,
in the silence of pastures and by riverbanks,
sound their clunky bells while grazing on
fresh grass, be where it might... She would stumble.
Her muzzle strikes the time-worn trough
15   and she recoils at the affront; but comes back,
brings her mouth to the water, and calmly drinks.
She takes little, not very thirsty... Then, she
lifts her huge head and horns to the sky
in a gesture that is grand and tragic; she bats
20   her lids over sightless pupils and turns away,
orphaned of light, beneath a burning sun,
lumbering up and down paths unforgettable,
dangling droopily her long-drawn tail.

EXCÈLSIOR

Vigila, esperit, vigila,
no perdis mai el teu nord;
no et deixis dur a la tranquil·la
aigua mansa de cap port.

5   Gira, gira els ulls enlaire,
no miris les platges roïns;
dóna el front an el gran aire,
sempre, sempre mar endins.

Sempre amb les veles suspeses
10   del cel al mar transparent;
sempre entorn aigües esteses
que es moguin eternament.

Fuig-ne, de la terra immoble,
fuig dels horitzons mesquins;
15   sempre al mar, al gran mar noble,
sempre, sempre mar endins.

Fora terra, fora platja,
oblidat de tot regrés:
no s'acaba el teu viatge,
20   no s'acabarà mai més.

EXCELSIOR

Keep watch, spirit, keep watch,
keep your compass to your star;
beware being drawn to the calm
subdued waters of harbors.

5   Turn, turn your eyes outward,
away from the paltry beaches;
your face to the open air,
out to the sea's farthest reaches.

Always your sails unrolled
10   from sky to limpid sea;
always waters stretching untold,
stirring, stirring eternally.

Fly from the standstill land,
fly, its horizons are meager;
15   set sail on the noble expanse,
out to the sea's farthest reaches.

Away, land and beach behind,
oblivious to all returning:
there is no end in sight,
20   there's to be no end to your journey.

FROM VISIONS & SONGS
(*VISIONS & CANTS*, 1900)

During the five years separating *Poesies* (1895) and *Visions & Cants* (1900), Maragall's stature grew as both poet and widely read opinion columnist for the *Diario de Barcelona*, coupled with his cultural activism as literary critic, translator, lecturer, and secretary of the Ateneu Barcelonès (see Casals 1998, 209-210). Certainly the best-known and most widely cited and scrutinized among Maragall's works (Abrams 2010, 121), *Visions & Cants* was not an overnight triumph, selling during the first year only some fifty of a 500-copy printing, though the edition sold out in a few years' time (Casals, 211).

The book is divided into three sections: *Visions*, with five poems, each dealing with a different legendary figure looming large in popular Catalan lore, and in one case, the larger-than-life historical figure of Catalano-Aragonese monarch Jaume I (r. 1213-1276); *Intermezzo*, with fourteen poems stemming from various seasonal and liturgical feasts marking the cyclical passage of time; and *Cants*, with eight poems drawing their symbolic strength largely from commonly shared historical and cultural experience specific to Catalan society and its struggle for survival and recognition as a peripheral linguistic community overshadowed by centripetal forces of monocultural stamp. The question of human identity, Abrams notes (121-124), runs through the poems in myriad ways, and Maragall puts a modern spin on traditional representations and their significance against a backdrop of growing social and cultural complexity. The poems spotlight individual and collective identities in vital contact, both contradictory and complementary, and the poet's voice leads the way in seeking a synthesis between old and new, real and ideal, self and other. Moreta (2010, 145-147) has argued the importance of the somewhat underreckoned second section, *Intermezzo* (unbilled in the volume's title), as the point of entry by way of reflection on everyday living into the broader questions raised about past and future in the limelighted *Visions* and *Cants* sections.

A striking example of Maragall's innovative and streamlined poetics can be seen in his treatment of the Germanic Arthurian tale versified by Gottfried August Bürger (1747-1794) as "Der Wilde Jäger," translated into English by Walter Scott (1771-1832) as "The Wild Huntsman" (first published as "The Chase" in 1796) and into French by Gérard de Nerval (1808-1855) and also put to music as the symphonic poem *Le Chasseur maudit* (1882) by César Franck (1822-1890). The appearance of the Catalan poem "Lo mal caçador" in *La Veu del Montserrat* (12 January 1895) by Joan Aliberch i Tort (1874-?) also served as springboard for Maragall's remarkable poem "El mal caçador" ("The Impious Hunter"), awarded the Viola d'Or i d'Argent (Gold and Silver Violet) prize for the best poetic composition of religious or moral significance at Barcelona's Jocs Florals in 1896 (see Casals 1998, 235-237). Abrams describes the poem's creative use of tradition as prototypical of modern poetics (2010, 127) and the tercets themselves, each with its unrhymed third verse, shun the fulfillment of the traditional ear while mirroring the triangular deployment of the poem's key elements: the host rising ever-upward and the hunter circling ever-horizontally below after the hare, a fitting scenography for the life-of-the-spirit versus life-of-the-flesh dilemma underlying the poem—and for Maragall's powerfully imaged refusal here, as elsewhere, to sever the twain. Similarly, Moreta, while noting that the transgression of impiety has occurred, finds conciliation—not condemnation—signaled in the poem's last four lines, where the sudden appearance of a quatrain throws up an accessory road sign. Moreta concludes:

The Impious Hunter has opted to follow the "devilish" hare, but that does not rule out his seeing God. Is not condemnation, according to the most genuine Church tradition, the privation of seeing God? If the Hunter "sees [the rising host] year after year" […] are we really talking about a character who has been condemned? (2010, 157)

In contrast to *El comte Arnau*, then, the question of punishment and redemption, Moreta suggests (156), may well be irrelevant to Maragall's uncanny rendering of the legendary hunter's impiety. Instead, the focus of poetic inquiry shifts to individual encounter with the Godhead, anticipating Maragall's article "The Church After Burning," where the partial destruction of the temple opens the way to encountering the divine.

El comte Arnau (Count Arnau) is a long poem of nearly one thousand lines composed over some fourteen years and published in three stages: the first part in *Visions & Cants* (1900—subsequent to its publication the same year in the literary magazine *Catalònia*), the second part in *Enllà* (1906), and the third and final part in *Seqüències* (1911). The origin of the legend of Count Arnau [pronounced: *are now*] has been traced to a popular ballad from the Ripoll area dating from the late sixteenth century, several versions of which have been collected (see Romeu 2000, 7-15). Arnau's ghost appears to his widow, Elvira, who learns that her husband's soul has been condemned because he cheated his laborers out of their wages. The legend's mythification and widespread appeal, however, gathers strength from Arnau's identification in popular lore with the dissolution by the pope in 1017 of the community of Benedictine nuns at the Monastery of Sant Joan de les Abadesses near Ripoll: the legendary Arnau is said to have famously seduced an abbess. The prolific literary and musical re-creation of the Arnau legend since the mid-nineteenth century in dozens of verse, prose, theatrical and musical works (see Romeu 2000, 12-15) has made Arnau Catalonia's most popular traditional rebel-hero icon (along with the early seventeenth-century *bandoler* Joan de Serrallonga; see the poem "The End of Serrallonga" in this selection).

Included here is the third and longest of the ten sections in the first part of *El comte Arnau*; selections from part two and part three appear under *Enllà* (1906) and *Seqüències* (1911), respectively, the volumes in which they were first published. In this section the poet makes us privy to the dialogue between Count Arnau and Adalaisa, a legendary abbess of Sant Joan de les Abadesses, in which Arnau seeks to win Adalaisa's compliance with his sensual designs. At first fruitless, Arnau's efforts will meet with success later when he steals into her cell through an underground tunnel and carries her off into the night; awaiting a child from the encounter, Adalaisa will be abandoned by Arnau: "Arnau, if I was yours, were you not mine?" // "Mine only are my arms and footfall" (Part One, IX). As Arthur Terry observes, "in part one there are certain echoes of Nietzsche, especially the three fragments of *Zarathustra* that Maragall himself translated" (2000, 23); Arnau's remarks on the heavens (III, 35-38) recall the opening lines of *Zarathustra* (24), and Arnau's reply to the "voices of the earth" (VI, not included in this selection) convey his desire "to be overman [*sobrehome*], / to be the throbbing earth."

Joan de Serrallonga, or Serrallonga, is the popular name given to the widely admired Catalan *bandoler* Joan Sala i Ferrer (1594-1634), whose legendary exploits as a plebs-loving outlaw have inspired dozens of literary, theatrical and musical works by writers and composers ranging from Toledo-born playwright Francisco de Rojas Zorrilla (1607-1648) and many more right up to the Catalan-television miniseries *Serrallonga, la llegenda del bandoler* (directed by Esteve Rovira, 2008). Maragall's 151-line poem—a dramatic monologue in which Serrallonga confesses his sins just before his execution in Barcelona on 8 January 1634—has been called one of his "most perfect and most extraordinary artistic creations" (Abrams 2010, 139). On Abrams's reading, Maragall's masterful rendering of Serrallonga's sacramental litany—enumerating his lifelong abandon to the seven deadly sins—brings the reader face-to-face with all the ambiguity and moral relativism of the human condition:

> Maragall wanted [...] us to discover [this] moral ambiguity and ambivalence, and to seriously question absolute and intransigent moral values. He had already done so [...] and invites us to undergo the same process. [Moral lines] are not so sharply drawn; they are relative and complex. The poem is extremely bold, powerful, and groundbreaking. (141)

The question of the sincerity of Serrallonga's confession and whether it complies with ecclesiatical dogma is resolved in the bomb-dropping final line. It is again Abrams who points out how Serrallonga's final request—that he might recite the articles of faith of the Apostles' Creed before the executioner brings down the axe—includes only up to article eleven (I believe in the resurrection of the flesh), that is, excluding the twelfth, and thereby refusing to embrace belief in everlasting life. In other words, Serrallonga's faith lies in the life of the flesh, not the soul: "where the flesh ends, so ends the faith of the legendary outlaw" (145). Structurally, the poem is deployed to a tee: including sixteen lines devoted to each of the outlaw's greatest sins (pride, wrath, envy and greed), twenty-four to his lesser faults (sloth, gluttony and lust), and sixteen more to the rebuttal in which he argues that his extramarital bond with Joana stemmed from love, not lust.

The short poem "En la mort d'un jove" ("At a Young Man's Death") is an elegy, composed shortly after Maragall's brother-in-law, Guillem ("Willie") Noble, died on 1 October 1895 at twenty-one years of age; an active athlete and enthusiastic hunter, Willie succumbed to tuberculosis following extreme athletic exertion and exhaustion (see Casals 1998, 305, 307). Abrams remarks how Maragall's treatment depicts death as "one more experience in life to be lived to the full":

Death and its accompanying conditions are, in effect, complementary to what Willie's life has been, the other side of the coin of the young athlete's life. In a word, Willie, through his death, is completing his life's trajectory. (2010, 157-158)

Also worthy of note here, as Moreta points out, is Maragall's innovative use of nature: the beauty of the sunset "moves the poet" despite the grief death brings, thus breaking with the notion of "nature as objective correlate of human feelings" and endowing nature with "an autonomy [not found] in the love poems of the *Claror* cycle sprung from [the poet's] courtship with Clara Noble" (2010, 151). Finally, the poem stands in interpretive contrast to its thematic counterpoint

"November Song" (see below).

The disarmingly irreverent short poem "Dimecres de Cendra" ("Ash Wednesday") serves as the point of entry for Moreta's (2010) exhaustive study of thought and religion in Joan Maragall. Encapsulated in just thirteen lines—most of these compressed into hexasyllables—is all the vitalistic force of Maragall's categorical rejection of the "language of mortification" (12) which, when brandished by ecclesiastical ritual and dogma, stands in the way of living:

We are not here to recall that we will die. We do not live to die. Being must not be the constant remembrance of non-being. Not even the occasional remembrance, one day a year, of non-being. Not even Ash Wednesday. No. We are not here to recall our human limits, nor to call to mind the smallness of our condition, nor to meditate on the fleeting character of existence. (12-13)

In the original, the more grammatically versatile Catalan "no" (both a sentential and absolute negator) occurs seven times in the thirteen-line poem (hat-tippingly matched by Moreta in the original Catalan of his own text quoted above). The seven "nos" operate as "the negation of a negation, ergo affirmation" (13), where Maragall's affirmation of living stands in opposition to "the predication of death [that would have us] renounce life" (15). Similarly, Casals notes how the poem is about "refusing to die while living, the rejection of restrictions and mortifications that are grave offenses against the joy of living" (1998, 315). (We might also note here that among Maragall's numerous translations of songs and hymns from the German is Friedrich Schiller's [1759-1805] *An die Freude* [Ode to Joy, 1785], rendered into Catalan as "Cant de joia" [1900], and upon which the final movement of Ludwig von Beethoven's [1770-1827] Ninth

Symphony [1824] is famously based.) Abrams's analysis (2010, 163-166) divides the poem into two parts: the poet's appeal to the young woman that she avoid the ritual placing of the ashes on the forehead (lines 1-8) and his statement regarding her proper place in the natural cycle of living (lines 9-13).

The extraordinary popularity of "El cant de la Senyera" ("Song to the Catalan Flag") stems from the strength of its symbolic role as a Catalan national anthem, put to music by composer Lluís Millet i Pagès (1867-1941) and first performed in 1896 at Montserrat Abbey during the solemn ceremony of the blessing of the Catalan flag. Originally written as a hymn for the association of choirs known as the Orfeó Català (co-founded by Millet in 1891), the song's triumph has obscured its authorship as it "continues to be sung as if it were an anonymous composition of traditional origin" (Casals 1998, 352). Banned under the dictatorships of Miguel Primo de Rivera (r. 1923-1929) and Francisco Franco (r. 1939-1975), it was on 19 May 1960 that "El cant de la Senyera" was sung at the Palau de la Música Catalana by members of the audience in an act of civil disobedience on the occasion of the centennial of Maragall's birth; the act of disobedience led to several arrests, including Jordi Pujol i Soley (b. 1930, president of the Generalitat de Catalunya, 1980-2003), who was tried by a military tribunal and sentenced to seven years' imprisonment, of which he served three and a half (see Casals 1998, 356). Abrams notes the skill with which the poet sustains the emotive intensity of a poem destined to symbolize a people and their struggle: "The flag of a people, such as the Catalan flag, symbolically embodies the values and aspirations of an entire community, which Maragall was able to detect and communicate to perfection" (2010, 196).

"Cant de novembre" ("November Song"), described by Abrams (203) as "the most direct and unequivocal expression of vitalism in Joan Maragall," is one of three poems in the section titled *Cants* that stands apart from the thread of historical and cultural legacy running through the rest—the other two are "Cant dels joves" (Song of Youth) and "Cant de maig, cant d'alegria" (Song of May, Song of Joy). Categorical in its affirmation of living beset by encroaching death, the poem's thematic kinship with "En la mort d'un jove" and "Dimecres de Cendra" lies in its "exaltation of joy, strength, pleasure, and life" (see Moreta 2010, 170).

The troubling events that unfolded with the collapse of Spanish colonialism in Cuba, Puerto Rico and the Philippines sparked concern and reflection that Maragall articulated both in numerous articles in the Barcelona press and in the trilogy of three short poems concluding *Visions & Cants*: "Els adéus" ("The Good-byes"), "Oda a Espanya" ("Ode to Spain") and "Cant del retorn" ("Song of Return"), collectively titled *Els tres cants de la guerra* (Three Songs of War). The extent of the folly and cost in human lives to the colonial cause of Spanish political and military involvement has been noted by Casals:

[...] Catalan participation in the intermittent Cuban wars had begun in 1868 when the Diputació de Barcelona organized and equipped a battalion of volunteers that sailed for Havana in 1869. The disastrous outcome of this first expedition (of 3600 troops shipped, only 369 remained by 1877) was premonitory of subsequent results: by November 1897 only 53,300 of the 200,000 men sent by the Spanish government in the preceding two years survived. (1998, 377 n. 7)

Yet beyond the particular historical circumstance that gave rise to the poems, there lives on in Maragall's art a universal appeal as well, a vital core upon which shared human experience is imprinted and which is transferable to other peoples and times. Analogously, Maragall points out how he discovered, while reading *The Persians* by Aeschylus, striking parallels between the denouement of the Greco-Persian Wars and the fall of Spanish colonialism in the Antilles and the Philippines (Maragall [1904a] 1960, 275; Casals 1998, 367-368; Abrams 2010, 210).

In "Els adéus," the juxtaposition of the wartime good-byes at the docks and that "first good-bye" of Cain's raises the ethical stakes of the poem through Christian allegory, ratcheting up the tension between martial duty and moral reflection. As Abrams points out in his careful analysis of the poem, Maragall underscores the absurdity of sending innocent young men "to kill and be killed in order to fulfill the will of the real Cain of the poem"—humanity's tendency toward violence; and the fact that "ships full of Abels [who] are sent off to act as Cains" will make their eventual return as Cains all the more senseless and distressing (2010, 213). The verbal and visual signs of separation—the good-byes—occur several times in the poem, including the title; prefiguring, as Abrams notes (211), the forceful ending of the second poem, "Oda a Espanya." In the poem's final image, however, with "the hands that moved in the air / to no avail, and that got no answer," the sign is now separated from its meaning: reduced to a mere motion of the hands, unacknowledged; resulting in the dramatic climax that heightens the pathos of separation bereft of any emotional or spiritual solace—a separation, in effect, without good-byes.

Ricard Torrents has remarked how, in the climactic final line to the poem "Oda a Espanya," Maragall rejects "the fitting together of the Catalan cultural nation with that of Spain" (Torrents 2011, 315). In this high-powered anti-ode, Maragall "finds himself unable to write a laudatory ode in the classic fashion" and so, faced with the unacceptable alternative of "moral and public hypocrisy," he is "obliged to tell the truth" (Abrams 2010, 215). In synthesis, this amounts to writing an apostrophic poem, addressing in "a language that isn't Spanish" (line 2) a Spain which, paradoxically, is nowhere to be seen—all the while depicting the terrible failure of Spain personified as a mother tragically alienated from her children. The paradox of Spain's absence, of course, is that the culturally and linguistically variegated Spain of Maragall's convivial ideal, that is, the real Spain, has been supplanted by an aggressive monoculture afflicted with cultural and linguistic daltonism. In the penultimate stanza Maragall urges Mother Spain to "think of the life that thrives all around you" and "smile at the sevenfold colors arching the clouds," that is, to embrace her multiple identity; but even as the poet holds out hope for reconciliation, in the final stanza Spain is no longer in sight. It is the Spain of reconciliation that is no longer present—as if the one who has broken the bond and gone away is not Mother Spain's children but Mother Spain herself. The choreography of the final farewell is one in which the poet and the peripheral culture he represents are standing in place; it is Spain that walks away (see Puppo 2012b, 223).

The immediate backdrop to the final poem of the trilogy, "Cant del retorn," was the returning home of Spain's defeated troops, begun in September 1898, two months before the actual signing of the Treaty of Paris that would put an end to the Spanish-American War (see Casals 1998, 384-385). After four stanzas describing the mournful homecoming from defeat abroad, what turns the poem around in the last two stanzas is the glimmer of hope that the language of the land—Catalan—lives on: "say whether the words we'll be using to bring / tears to her eyes are living, or have died." The dramatic, optimistic upturn at the poem's end underscores the language as the key to sustaining the collective life of the peripheral

linguistic community to which, and for which, the poet speaks—
living words for a living people. Finally, highlighting the concluding
upturn is the poem's very title: "Cant del retorn." Besides denoting
the poem itself—the greater part of which is a song of sorrow—it
also signals, more specifically, the poem's final image: the song of
joy to which the song of tears and sorrow has given way. Further, as
the final poem not only of the trilogy but also of the entire volume
Visions & Cants, the poem's concluding imperative "Let go a laugh
and break out in song!" acquires enhanced discursive force as its
context widens beyond the confines of the poem and the book,
calling readers, as Abrams (2010, 223) points out, to "take up again
the great cycle of life."

EL MAL CAÇADOR

La missa matinal
la diuen allà dalt
aixís que es fa de dia.

La missa de l'estiu
5 el capellà la diu
amb les portes obertes.

S'oeix de tots costats
quan enflaira els serrats
el ginestar de Corpus.

10 El caçador es deleix.
De fora estant l'oeix
amb un genoll en terra.

Al bell punt d'alçar Déu,
li bota allí, al bell peu,
15 la llebre endiastrada.

S'esventa el gos lladrant,
la llebre fuig botant,
i el caçador al darrera.

«Corres i correràs,
20 mai més t'aturaràs».
Aquesta és la sentència.

«Doncs, corro i correré,
mai més m'aturaré.

THE IMPIOUS HUNTER

Morning rites are held
up there on the hill
just as day is breaking.

During summertime
5   the priest conducts the rite
with chapel doors flung open.

Prayers from inside rise
to slopes of broom nearby
all fragrant for the Corpus.

10   Bursting at the seams,
the hunter bends a knee
to hear the holy words.

Godhead lifted high,
a hare comes by—
15   devilish and wild at his feet.

Up bolts yelping hound,
hare away in a bound
and hunter fast on their heels.

"Fast! Fast on the track!
20   Nothing to hold you back!"
That is the sentence served.

"Yes! Forever fast on the track!
Nothing to hold me back!

Alegre és la sentència».

25 S'allunyen amb el vent,
perdent-se en un moment
els crits, la fressa, el rastre…

Passen dies i nits…
Pels marges reflorits
30 ha tornat Corpus Christi.

La missa matinal
la diuen allà dalt:
les portes són obertes.

En un vent de visió
35 passa el mal caçador
entre lladrucs i fressa.

Se gira i veu l'altar,
i al peu el capellà,
i en alt veu l'hòstia càndida.

40 Passa i es perd al lluny…
La boirina del juny
cenyeix l'horitzó immòbil.

Roden les estacions,
revénen els plançons:
45 cada any, cada any ve Corpus.

Cada any torna a passar,
cada any torna a mirar,
cada any, la missa augusta.

Happy the sentence served!"

25 Off they fly on the wind—
and very next instant
the clamor and chase fade out…

The days and nights roll by…
till there on the flowering heights
30 it's Corpus Christi once more.

Morning rites are held
up there on the hill
the chapel doors flung open.

In a wind of vision
35 amid the howl and din
the impious hunter goes by.

Turning now he sees
the altar, and the priest
and shining Host raised high.

40 He fades into the distance…
where June's mistiness
envelops the still horizon.

Seasons turn and turn,
saplings once more burgeon,
45 and year after year comes Corpus.

Each year the hunter goes by,
each year he catches sight
once more of the holy rite.

Cada any els capellans
50 tenen més cabells blancs
i aixequen més els braços.

Cada any l'hòstia es va alçant,
el temple es va aixafant
i l'hòstia puja, puja…

55 Passen més anys i més,
el capellà no hi és:
l'hòstia va sola en l'aire.

Amunt, amunt, amunt…
La volta perd el junt,
60 la llum del cel s'hi filtra.

L'hòstia s'hi va acostant,
el temple es va esquerdant…
El caçador no para.

Ve un any…, la volta cau
65 i s'obre el gran cel blau
damunt de l'hòstia blanca

que s'alça lentament…
Al ser l'estiu vinent,
floreix el temple en runes.

70 Se'n va pujant al cel…
El caçador amb anhel
cada any, cada any la mira.

L'hòstia per 'nar al zenit,
té l'espai infinit,

Each year the priests presiding
50   show hair ever-whitening
and lift their arms yet higher.

Each year the Host keeps rising,
the temple meanwhile declining...
as the Host lifts higher and higher...

55   Seasons turn, on and on—
all the priests now gone...
the Host rises alone.

Higher and higher and higher...
Stonework torn and tired,
60   the sunlight filters through.

The Host now nears the vault,
beneath the cracks and faults...
Round and round the hunter goes.

One year, the vault collapses—
65   and the sky's blue expanse
opens before the Host,

and slowly, slowly, it rises...
Come summertime,
the temple blooms in ruins.

70   In the sky the Host rises...
The hunter sees and sighs
year after year, and longs.

The Host on its road to the sky
has no end of space.

75   i ell, per caçar, encisat,
     té el temps, l'eternitat.

75   And the wistful hunter for the chase,
     no end of time.

FROM EL COMTE ARNAU

(PRIMERA PART: EL COMTE ARNAU)

III

—Treu-te la capa —li demana ella—.
Treu-te la capa, que et veuré més gran.
25   —Treu-te tu el manto, que et veuré més bella.
—No, que só l'abadessa de Sant Joan—.

Canta una alosa de la part de fora,
per la finestra entra el sol brillant,
el cel és blau, i resplendenta l'hora:
30   el comte i l'abadessa es van mirant.

—Treu-te tu el manto, que et veuré més bella:
sense toca et voldria i sense vel.
—De genolls jo et voldria en la capella:
tan gloriós, faries goig al cel.

35   —Pro a mi el cel no em fa goig més que si el miro
des de la terra sobre meu obert:
me plau trobar-lo, quan els ulls hi giro,
buit i silenciós com un desert.

El cel és el repòs de la mirada,
40   i és el repòs del braç i el pensament;
per'xò, ajagut a terra, el cel m'agrada
i m'adormo mirant-lo fixament.

—Altre cel és per mi la tenebrosa
capella on un altar brilla tot sol:

FROM COUNT ARNAU

(PART ONE: COUNT ARNAU)

III

"Remove your cloak," she suggests.
"Go on, bring out your greatness."
25   "Remove your mantle, bring out your loveliness."
"Not likely. This is Sant Joan, I am the abbess."

Somewhere a skylark sings outside,
Through a window sunlight plays,
The skies are blue, the hour bright:
30   As count and abbess meet each other's gaze.

"Remove your mantle, bring out your loveliness:
I'd have you without wimple, shed the veil."
"And you I'd have on your knees in the chapel:
So glorious, you'd bring such delight to heaven."

35   "The only delight the heavens bring me
Is when spread out above me over the earth:
Lifting my gaze to them, that's when I see
How empty and silent they seem like a desert.

"The skies are rest for the eyes,
40   And rest for the arms, and the mind;
As I lie on the earth the heavens delight me
And bring me restful sleep for a time."

"A different heaven is for me the shadowy
Chapel, where all alone the altar shines:

45   el cos humiliat sobre una llosa,
l'ànima deslliurada aixeca el vol.

I de la terra i d'aquest món s'oblida,
sospirant per la mort que ha de venir.
—En tos llavis gruixuts, de mort al dir,
50   com hi oneja suaument la vida!

—Mes són fang. Quan per sempre s'hauran clos,
vindran els cucs i se'n faran pastura.
Vull amagrir els meus llavis i el meu cos
per fer-me tornar l'ànima més pura—.

55   Canta una alosa de la part de fora,
per la finestra entra el sol brillant,
el cel és blau i resplendenta l'hora:
el comte i l'abadessa es van mirant.

—Adalaisa, tu que ets tan vividora
60   i que els ulls els tens plens de voluntat,
i aquesta àvida boca prenedora,
i en els teus aires tanta majestat,

¿com és que ara malparles de la vida,
per la que estàs tan fortament armada?
65   No t'escau la mirada esmortuïda
sota l'arc de la cella ben poblada.

Escaurà bé a tes pàl·lides germanes,
tristos cossos per sempre immaternals:
per elles són les fantasies vanes
70   de vagues resplendors celestials.

45   The body humbled there on the flagstones,
      The soul, unfettered, takes to the skies.

      "And there the earth and this world—it forgets,
      And longs for the death that is to come."
      "How softly life comes flowing from
50   Your fleshy lips now speaking death!"

      "They are but clay. Once closed forever,
      The worms will come and have their day.
      Thin lips and frame would suit me better
      To help me make my soul more chaste."

55   Somewhere a skylark sings outside,
      Through a window sunlight plays,
      The skies are blue, the hour bright:
      As count and abbess meet each other's gaze.

      "Adalaisa, you who are so full of life,
60   Whose eyes give off that eager glow,
      Whose willing lips were made to invite,
      Whose grace and majesty were meant to show,

      "How can it be you shrug off life,
      For which you are so well fit out?
65   Not for you are somber eyes
      Below your full and shapely brow.

      "That may suit your pallid sisters,
      Sad frames forever unmaternal:
      For them the fleeting gleam and glitter
70   Of promises eternal.

Però tu, performada criatura,
delícia de la terra, torna al món!
Romp el cordó que injuria ta cintura!
Arrenca't, Adalaisa, els vels del front!—

75 I avança Arnau hermosament; pro es gira
airosa ella an el Sant Cristo nu,
i signant-lo an el comte, li diu: —Mira:
aquest encara és més hermós que tú!—

Canta una alosa de la part de fora,
80 per la finestra entra el sol brillant,
el cel és blau i resplendenta l'hora:
el comte i l'abadessa es van mirant.

"But you, creature so finely made,
Come back to the world, earthly delight!
Break the cord that wrongs your waist!
Adalaisa, throw your veils aside!"

75 And Arnau, handsome, draws near; but she turns
gracefully to the Holy Christ, nude,
and points to Him and speaks these words:
"Look! He's even more handsome than you!"

Somewhere a skylark sings outside,
80 Through a window sunlight plays,
The skies are blue, the hour bright:
As count and abbess meet each other's gaze.

LA FI D'EN SERRALLONGA

—Pare, absoleu-me: só cansat de viure.
—T'escomet a bona hora el cansament.
La teva via s'ha acabat i ets lliure
d'anar-te'n al repòs eternalment.

5   Mes, abans d'adormir-te i reposar-te,
cal que et recordis dels teus grans pecats:
tots aquells que jo puga perdonar-te,
també de Déu seran-te perdonats.

—El primer pecat meu és l'orgull, pare:
10   jo só aquell que he tingut un rei al cos;
mai he pogut sofrir que algú em manara:
fer la llei a tot déu era el meu goig.
Per'xò he tingut tant odi al rei d'Espanya
i li he fet la guerra jo tot sol.

15   Ell la terra ens ha omplert de gent estranya
i manar-nos-ho tot és lo que vol.
Doncs, jo li he dit: «No em plau!» I, via fora!
he anat pel món com m'ha vingut a pler,
he fet lo que he volgut, lliure a tothora,

20   i no he obeït llei, ni rei, ni re.
I, tant se val!, és una bella cosa
fer tremolar a tothom i estar segur!
Cap respecte en ma via m'ha fet nosa,
mai he baixat la testa per ningú…
—Mes ara…

25   —Mes ara, que ja sé que compareixo
en presència de Déu omnipotent…

THE END OF SERRALLONGA

"Father, forgive me, for I have grown weary of living."
"Your weariness comes in good season.
Your road has reached its end and you are free
to go and rest eternally.

5   But before you sleep that sleep,
you must recall your greatest sins:
all those it lies in my power to forgive you
will by God be forgiven too."
"The first of my sins is pride, Father:

10   I have lodged a prince within my body;
never could I suffer being governed by another:
in commanding all others I relished no end.
I detested for this reason the king of Spain
and all alone waged war against him.

15   He has put our land in strangers' hands
and would have us do his bidding in all.
So I piped up: 'I won't have it!' And to arms!
I have walked the world to my own delight,
I have done what pleased me, every instant free,

20   bending to no law, no king, no thing.
And just as well! How marvelous it is
putting all to tremble—yet stand unscathed!
Respect at my passing was never a nuisance,
nor ever did I bow before any…"
"But now…"

25   "But now that I know I've been summoned
to appear before God the Almighty…"

—Te'n penedeixes?

    —Sí, me'n penedeixo.

—Doncs, sia't perdonat.

    —Amén, amén…

—Quin altre pecat tens?

    —La ira, pare.

30   Quan m'encenc no tinc fre ni aturador,
me giro contra el món, Déu i sa Mare,
i tot voldria dur-ho a destrucció.
Pare, he estat cruel: moltes vegades
m'he delitat vegent rajar la sang;
35   he vist alçar-se a mi mans ajuntades
i segar-se genolls caient al fang.
I jo me n'he rigut, perquè em plavia,
i, podent perdonar, no he perdonat…
És una cosa dolça i fa alegria
40   veure un 'nemic als peus ben manillat!
I fer mal! I fer mal! Allò era viure:
destruir sols per gust i per voler,
sentir plorar a tothom i poder riure…
Ser com rei de dolor… És bell, a fe!
45   —Fill meu! Fill meu! Això és massa malesa;
això és un mal esprit que tens al cos:
encara en parles amb la vista encesa,
en foc d'infern!…

    —No, no!… Ja ve el repòs.

Doncs, ara que ja sé que compareixo
50   en presència de Déu omnipotent…

    —Te'n penedeixes?

"You are heartily sorry?"

    "Yes, I am heartily sorry."

"Then thou art forgiven."

    "Amen, amen…"

"What other sins have you?"

    "Wrath, Father.

30   When I get fired up there's no stopping or holding me back,

I strike out at the world, God and Holy Mother,

and would smash all things to pieces.

Father, I have been cruel: many a time

I've taken delight in seeing the blood spill,

35   and hands raised to me clasping for clemency

and knees bent low in the mud.

And I laughed it off: because it was my pleasure,

and when it was in my power to pardon, I did not…

'Tis a sweet and wondrous thing

40   to see an enemy bound at your feet.

And strike! And strike again! Now that was living:

to destroy for the sheer thrill of it,

hear all others cry and yet laugh…

To be prince of pain… 'Tis lovely, truly!"

45   "My son! This wickedness goes too far:

a demon dwells in your body;

even as you speak your eyes smolder

with the sulfurs of hell!"…

    "No! Eternal rest!

Now that I know I've been summoned

50   to appear before God the Almighty…"

    "You are heartily sorry?"

—Sí, me'n penedeixo.

—Doncs, sia't perdonat.

—Amén, amén…

—També he tingut enveja i mala bava
per corrompre la glòria dels demés:
55 allí on jo he conegut que no arribava,
no he volgut que cap altre hi arribés.
D'aquell que em feia ombra o bé respecte,
m'he gaudit fent-ne córrer males veus,
i, tot fingint-li acatament i afecte,
60 li anava segant l'herba sota els peus.
De lo que no he entès n'he dit mentida,
dels fets més grans que els meus, n'he dit rampells,
he volgut sols un pes, sols una mida:
la meva: els que en passaven, pobres d'ells!
65 Rebaixar, rebaixar, fins que es confonga
tothom en un mesquí i humil estol,
i al damunt en Joan Sala i Serrallonga,
sent més que tots i governant tot sol.

—Mes, ara…

—Mes, ara que ja sé que compareixo
70 en presència de Déu omnipotent…

—Te'n penedeixes?

—Sí, me'n penedeixo.

—Doncs, sia't perdonat.

—Amén, amén…

—He estat avar: mai he tingut de sobra,
sempre he anat per més al camí ral;
75 per molt que posseís, sentia'm pobre

"Yes, I am heartily sorry."
"Then thou art forgiven."
"Amen, amen…"

"I have also harbored envy, and a malicious tongue
in subverting the glory of others:
55   that which I knew was beyond my grasp,
I took steps to secure no one else could achieve.
Of those who dimmed my luster or stood out,
I relished in spreading vicious rumors,
and feigning my affection and support,
60   I sapped their strength and plotted their demise.
Things I knew to be true I draped in lies,
and taller deeds than mine I snubbed as trifles;
for me, one weight, one measure only:
mine; and for those who neglected to notice, flowers!
65   Decry and belittle, till everyone's mingled
and mixed in a single, humble, miserable flock,
above which there rises Joan Sala i Serrallonga,
yours truly, fit like no other to govern alone."
"But now…"

     "But now that I know I've been summoned
70   to appear before God the Almighty…"
"You are heartily sorry?"
     "Yes, I am heartily sorry."
"Then thou art forgiven."
     "Amen, amen…"

"I have been greedy: I never had enough,
ever eager for more on life's highroad;
75   for all I possessed, I felt like a pauper,

i amb la por d'anar a raure a l'hospital.

Ai! La cobdícia no em deixava viure,

era roí pels altres i per mi:

per un parell de bous, per una lliura,

80 hauria fet deu hores de camí.

Veure'm diner apilat m'aconsolava,

mes fruir no podia'n altrament

que pensant a quants altres els mancava

allò que era per mi un bon passament.

85 «Això és ben meu —pensava—; això no falla;

els altres, si misèria o fam vingués,

que es pengin!» I, llavores, ni una malla

hauria dat a un pobre que passés.

—Mes, ara…

       —Mes, ara que ja sé que compareixo

90 en presència de Déu omnipotent…

—Te'n penedeixes?

       —Sí, me'n penedeixo.

—Doncs, sia't perdonat.

       —Amén, amén…

—La peresa, la gola i la luxúria

ben cert que foren mos pecats més xics;

95 pro algun cop m'ha plagut deixar la fúria

dels combats, lluny d'amics i d'enemics.

Me n'anava a fer cap a la masia

oblidada en el fons d'alguna vall,

i m'entaulava en bona companyia,

100 menyspreant tota lluita i tot treball.

Llavores jo me'n reia de la guerra

and dreaded I'd end up one day in the poorhouse.
My greediness kept me from living,
I was contemptible to others and myself:
for an ox or two, or a handful of coins,
80   I'd have traveled ten hours.
To see money piled up was my solace,
but I could never enjoy it, except
by thinking of how many others were lacking
in that which for me was a comfortable means.
85   'This,' I thought, 'is mine; it can't go wrong:
as for others, if poverty and hunger came knocking,
let 'em hang!' I wouldn't give so much
as a tuppence to a wandering beggar."
"But now…"
        "But now that I know I've been summoned
90   to appear before God the Almighty…"
"You are heartily sorry?"
        "Yes, I am heartily sorry."
"Then thou art forgiven."
        "Amen, amen…"

"Sloth, gluttony, lust:
these of course were my smaller sins;
95   but sometimes I took to leaving the fury
of combat, far from comrade or foe.
I'd seek out some solitary house
lost deep in a hollow somewhere,
and there I'd feast in good company,
100   shunning battles and labors.
Then I'd laugh outright at war,

i dels meus que es batien, capsigranys!,
i tant se me'n donava que la terra
la manessin els propis o els estranys.
105 Ben menjat, ben begut, plavia'm jeure
a bona ombra per fer la migdiada,
cantant cançons d'amor que fan distreure,
o escoltant els aucells en la brancada.
Si llavores passava alguna mossa
110 revinguda de cos, jo la cridava,
ella venia a mi, la deshonrava,
i encara se'n tenia per ditxosa.
—I goses riure?
       —Era cosa bona...
—Mes no ho és pas a l'hora de la mort.
115 —Bon menjar, bon oblit i jeure amb dona:
mai havia trobat millor conhort.
—Mes, ara...
       —Mes, ara que ja sé que compareixo
en presència de Déu omnipotent...
—Te'n penedeixes?
       —Sí, me'n penedeixo.
—Doncs, sia't perdonat.
120   —Amén, amén...

—I el tracte amb na Joana, no és injúria
que clama també a Déu Nostre Senyor?
Acusa't!...
       —Pare, no: no fou luxúria,
sinó una veritable estimació.
125 És cert que jo en ses carns moltes vegades

and my comrades back in the field, blockheads!
Nor could I care less if the land
was governed by ours or by theirs.

105 Filled with good food and good drink, I was glad
to lie down in the shade for an afternoon nap,
sing songs of love for amusement,
or hear the birds in the brier.
And if a handsome wench happened to pass,

110 healthy and robust, I'd call to her,
she'd come to me, I'd disgrace her,
and still she would count herself lucky."
"And you find this amusing?"
       "'Twas a fine thing…"
"Not so at the hour of your death."

115 "Good food, far from troubles, being with a woman:
never was there better comfort."
"But now…"
       "But now that I know I've been summoned
to appear before God the Almighty…"
"You are heartily sorry?"
       "Yes, I am heartily sorry."
"Then thou art forgiven."

120   "Amen, amen…"

"And that business with Joana, is it not an affront
clamoring to the Lord Our God for atonement?
Confess!…"
       "No, Father: it was not lust,
it was a true and real love.

125 Yes, many were the times I buried so much

hi he enterrat tant de força i de voler!

Mes eren llaç d'amor ses abraçades

i coronat de seny son front serè.

La Joana m'ha estat reina i esclava,

130 molts cops ella pensava per tots dos;

quan jo estava dormint, ella vetllava;

ella m'ha fet valent i poderós.

M'ha ajudat amb l'esguard, amb la paraula;

si ha calgut, amb la força del seu braç;

135 cada migdia m'ha llescat pa a taula

i cada vespre m'ha alegrat el jaç.

En paga, jo li ha estat amant sol·lícit…

D'això també me n'haig de penedir?

—Fou un amor desordenat i il·lícit!

140 —Doncs… tant se val!… me'n penedeixo, sí!

—Tens algun pecat més dins teu?

　　　—No, pare.

—De tots els que m'has dit, i els que has comès

contrit demanes perdó a Déu?

　　　—Sí, pare.

—I et sap greu de tot cor d'haver-lo ofès?

—Sí.

145 　　　—Doncs, en nom de Déu omnipotent,

Pare, Fill i Esperit Sant, t'absolc. Amén.

…………………………

—Moriré resant el credo;

mes digueu an el botxí

que no em mati fins i a tant

150 que m'hagi sentit a dir:

«Crec en la resurrecció de la carn».

strength and longing into her flesh!
Yet her embraces were the bonds of love
and reason crowned her brow serene.
My Joana was both slave and queen;
130 she often thought for both of us,
while I would sleep, she kept the watch;
she gave me nerve and sinew.
She did me good with every look and word;
if need be, with a strong arm too;
135 each noonday meal she sliced my bread,
and brought, each evening to my chamber, cheer.
In recompense, I've been an eager lover…
Must I be sorry for that too?"
"It was a wrong, unruly love!"
140 "Then so be it! I am heartily sorry, yes!"
"Keep you any other sins within?"
        "No, Father…"
"For all these you have told of and committed,
do you ask sincerely God's forgiveness?"
        "Yes, Father."
"And you are sorry with all your heart for offending Him?"
"Yes."
145   "Then in the name of God the Almighty,
Father, Son and Holy Spirit, I absolve you from your sins. Amen."

. . . .

"I will die with the credo on my lips;
but kindly instruct the deathsman first
that he not bring down the axe until
150 he hears that I have uttered these words:
'I believe in the resurrection of the flesh.' "

EN LA MORT D'UN JOVE

Te'n vas anar amb aquell ponent dolcíssim…
Caigueres, lluitador, al marxar a la lluita.
Somreies a la força dels teus muscles
i glaties per guerres i corones,
5   i tot de cop t'has esllanguit per terra
amb els ulls admirats…

Ai, la Mort, i que n'ets d'embellidora!
Aquell teu primer vel, quan el llançares
damunt de l'hèroe en flor, tots somriguérem
10   sota els plors estroncats, que una serena
va començar a regnar en el pit i el rostre
del moribond. L'alè anava i venia
suaument emperesit, fins que esperàrem…
I no tornà… Llavores esclataven
15   més alts els plors al cel… Ell ja no hi era…
Pro a fora, al camp, era un ponent dolcíssim.

AT A YOUNG MAN'S DEATH

You went away with that soft, soft sunset…
You fell, fighter, setting out for the fight.
How you smiled at the strength of your muscles
and how you longed for war and laurels,
5   then suddenly you lay drained on the ground,
your eyes astonished…

Death, how fine you do embellish!
That first veil of yours, when you spread it
over the flowering hero, we all smiled
10   beneath the spent tears, for a stillness
now set in and calmed the chest and visage
at your approach. The breathing in and out
slackened gently, while we waited…
And then it stopped… Then louder cries broke
15   and rose to the skies… Now he wasn't there…
But outside, on the fields, there shone a soft, soft sunset.

DIMECRES DE CENDRA

A UNA NOIA

No et facis posar cendra, — no et facis posar cendra,
        patró de joventut,
que no té res que veure — la mort, la cendra, amb tu.
        No entelis amb mementos
5   ton front rosat i pur.

Tu no has pas d'haver esment — de la trista paraula
        que diu el sacerdot
        girant-se de la taula.

Que aquest color rosat — que duus al front i als llavis
10 no t'ha sigut donat — per cendrosos agravis,

        que t'ha sigut donat,
        verge de la sang tendra,
per uns altres esblaims — que no són pols ni cendra.

ASH WEDNESDAY

TO A YOUNG WOMAN

Stay clear of those ashes, stay away from the ashes,
      custodian of youth,
death and ashes, you know, haven't the least bit to do with you.
      Don't let this token tarnish
5   your forehead rosy and fresh.

You needn't be acquainted with the gloomy phrase
      the priest will say
      when he turns your way.

The rich flush you show on your forehead and lips
10 wasn't given you for ashy affronts;

      it was given you,
      tender sanguine bud,
for other palettes, that are not ash or dust.

EL CANT DE LA SENYERA

Al damunt dels nostres cants
aixequem una Senyera
que els farà més triomfants.

Au, companys, enarborem-la
5   en senyal de germandat!
Au, germans, al vent desfem-la
en senyal de llibertat!
Que voleï! contemplem-la
en sa dolça majestat!

10   Oh bandera catalana!,
nostre cor t'és ben fidel;
volaràs com au galana
pel damunt del nostre anhel:
per mirar-te sobirana
15   alçarem els ulls al cel.

I et durem arreu enlaire,
et durem, i tu ens duràs:
voleiant al grat de l'aire,
el camí assenyalaràs.
20   Dóna veu al teu cantaire,
llum als ulls i força al braç.

SONG TO THE CATALAN FLAG

High above, above our hymns
up we raise a flag that waves
and will make our song more strong.

Hoist it high, companions,
5   this our sign of brotherhood!
Unfurl it, sisters and brothers, in the wind,
this our sign of freedom!
Let it fly! See how it
waves in gentle majesty!

10   O Catalan colors!
in you our hearts hold faith;
a great-winged bird, you fly
commanding every hope:
to see you in your sovereignty,
15   we lift our gazes to the sky.

We'll carry you ever high,
and you will carry us:
flying in the wind's grace,
you will show us the way.
20   Give voice to we who sing you,
light to our eyes and strength to our limbs.

CANT DE NOVEMBRE

El vermell dels arbres,
encès per la posta — dels sols hivernals,
    delita i penetra
lo mateix que aquells verds primaverals.
5   Germans, alcem els cors que tot és bell,
        el verd i el vermell!

Alcem els cors cantant la vida entera
amb els brots i amb les fulles que se'n van;
gosem el dia sens mirar endarrera,
10 sense pensar amb els dies que vindran.
        Gosa el moment;
        gosa el moment que et convida,
i correràs alegre a tot combat;
        un dia de vida és vida:
15 gosa el moment que t'ha sigut donat.
No t'entristeixin, doncs, els funerals novembres,
ni planyis mort lo que ha tingut ple ser…
De plànyer és el donzell que ajeu sos membres
ans d'haver-los cansat en el plaer.

NOVEMBER SONG

The red of the trees,
lit up by the setting winter suns,
  delights and penetrates
the same as the greens of spring.
5 Brothers and sisters, hearts be lifted, beauty pervades:
   in green and in red!

Our hearts be lifted singing life complete
with its buds and its leaves that fade away;
let's dare the day and not look back,
10 not think of days to come.
   Dare the moment;
   dare the moment inviting,
and you'll spring with gusto into every combat;
   one day of life is life:
15 dare the moment given you.
Don't grieve, then, these funeral Novembers,
nor lament the death of that which fully was…
Lament the young who put their limbs to rest
without first having tired them in delight.

ELS TRES CANTS DE LA GUERRA

ELS ADÉUS

Que senyals d'adéu han fet
mans esteses cap al mar,
vers els barcos que fugien
amb les cobertes massa carregades,
5   cap allà on les onades lluïen
retorcent-se i bramant assoleiades!

Quants adéus des d'aquell adéu primer,
quan Caí, havent fet la mort,
menjà al vespre un bocí a l'endiablada,
10   el bastó al puny, cenyida la cintura,
voltat de plors de nins, i la muller,
que li deia amb lament:
«No vagis cap a Ponent!»

Mes ell, la cara adusta i ja fatal
15   girada envers la posta,
marxà, no fent cabal
de les mans que es movien enlaire
en va, sense resposta.

THREE SONGS OF WAR

THE GOOD-BYES

Now those were good-byes, waving
hands reaching for the sea,
out to the ships pushing off,
with decks that were overfilled,
5   bound for glimmering sea-swells
twisting and wailing bright in the sun!

So many good-byes since that first good-bye,
when Cain, having given death,
ate little that evening, devilishly pressed,
10   gripping his staff and belt drawn tight,
circled by children's cries, and wife,
pleading:
"Don't go the road the sun takes!"

But he, grim-faced and resigned to his fate,
15   and turning to the sunken sun,
set out, striding past
the hands that moved in the air
to no avail, and that got no answer.

ODA A ESPANYA

Escolta, Espanya, — la veu d'un fill
que et parla en llengua — no castellana:
parlo en la llengua — que m'ha donat
la terra aspra;
5   en 'questa llengua — pocs t'han parlat;
en l'altra, massa.

T'han parlat massa — dels seguntins
i dels qui per la pàtria moren;
les teves glòries — i els teus records,
10   records i glòries — només de morts:
has viscut trista.

Jo vull parlar-te — molt altrament.
Per què vessar la sang inútil?
Dins de les venes — vida és la sang,
15   vida pels d'ara — i pels que vindran;
vessada, és morta.

Massa pensaves — en ton honor
i massa poc en el teu viure:
tràgica duies — a mort els fills,
20   te satisfeies — d'honres mortals
i eren tes festes — els funerals,
oh trista Espana!

Jo he vist els barcos — marxar replens
dels fills que duies — a que morissin:

ODE TO SPAIN

Hear me out, Spain, a son's voice
speaking a language that isn't Spanish:
I speak the language given me
by the rugged land;
5   few in such words have addressed you—
too many in others.

On and on they've gone about Saguntians
and those that died for *la patria*,
and your glories and your memories,
10   memories and glories: only of death—
you live in sadness.

I want to talk to you differently.
Why shed blood so needlessly?
In the veins blood is life,
15   life for those now, and those to come;
spilled, it dies.

So much thought about your honor,
so little about your living:
tragic, you shipped your sons away to die,
20   you fed yourself on honors post-mortem,
and funerals were your festivals,
sad Spain.

I've seen your ships shoving off, filled
with sons you ferried to their deaths:

25 somrients marxaven — cap a l'atzar;
    i tu cantaves — vora del mar
    com una folla.

    On són els barcos? — On són els fills?
    Pregunta-ho al Ponent i a l'ona brava:
30 tot ho perderes, — no tens ningú.
    Espanya, Espanya, — retorna en tu,
    arrenca el plor de mare!

    Salva't, oh!, salva't — de tant de mal;
    que el plor et torni feconda, alegre i viva;
35 pensa en la vida que tens entorn:
    aixeca el front,
    somriu als set colors que hi ha en els núvols.

    On ets, Espanya? — No et veig enlloc.
    No sents la meva veu atronadora?
40 No entens aquesta llengua — que et parla entre perills?
    Has desaprès d'entendre an els teus fills?
    Adéu, Espanya!

25 off they went, smiling, come what might,
    while there along the shore you sang
    like a madwoman.

    Where are those ships? those sons?
    Go ask the dropping sun and rolling waves—
30 you lost everything, have no one.
    Pull yourself together, Spain:
    let out the mother's cry!

    Get out from under all this pain.
    Your tears will turn you fertile, happy, alive;
35 think of the life that thrives all around you:
    lift up your face,
    and smile at the sevenfold colors arching the clouds.

    Where are you, Spain? I can't see you anywhere.
    Don't you hear my voice coming through?
40 Don't you grasp the speech I speak at risk?
    Have you unlearned your children's words?
    Adéu, Espanya!

CANT DEL RETORN

Tornem de batalles, — venim de la guerra,
i no portem armes, pendons ni clarins;
vençuts en la mar, — vençuts en la terra,
som una desferra.
5   Duem per estela taurons i dofins.
Germans que en la platja plorant espereu,
ploreu, ploreu!

Pel mar se us avança — la host malicenta
que branda amb el brand de la nau que la duu.
10   Adéu, oh tu, Amèrica, terra furienta!
Som dèbils per tu.
Germans que en la platja plorant espereu,
ploreu, ploreu!

Venim tots de cara — al vent de la costa,
15   encara que ens mati per fred i per fort,
encara que restin en sense resposta
més d'un crit de mare quan entrem al port.
Germans que en la platja plorant espereu,
ploreu, ploreu!

20   De tants com ne manquen duem la memòria
de lo que sofriren — de lo que hem sofert,
de la trista lluita sense fe ni glòria
d'un poble que es perd.
Germans que en la platja plorant espereu,
25   ploreu, ploreu!

SONG OF RETURN

We come home from battle, return from the war,
we carry no arms, no banners or bugles;
defeated at sea, defeated on land,
we come back in shambles,
5   with nothing but sharks and dolphins in tow.
Brothers and sisters, waiting in grief along the shore,
let go your tears.

Now steaming homeward, we haggard hosts
but brandish the glint of the ship that brings us.
10   Good-bye, Americas, wrathful lands!
To you we are weak.
Brothers and sisters, waiting in grief along the shore,
let go your tears.

We now set our faces to the coastal wind,
15   though it blast and freeze us to death,
and though coming to dock, more than one
mother's calling should raise no reply.
Brothers and sisters, waiting in grief along the shore,
let go your tears.

20   Of those who are absent we bring the memory
of all that they suffered, and all that we've suffered,
and the sorry struggle, faithless and unglorious,
of a lost and losing people.
Brothers and sisters, waiting in grief along the shore,
25   let go your tears.

Digueu-nos si encara la pàtria és prou forta
per oir les gestes — que li hem de contar;
digueu-nos, digueu-nos si és viva o si és morta
la llengua amb què l'haurem de fer plorar

30 Si encara és ben viu el record d'altres gestes,
si encara les serres que ens han d'enfortir
s'aixequen serenes damunt les tempestes
i bramen llurs boscos al vent ponentí,
germans que en la platja plorant espereu,
35 no ploreu: rieu, canteu!

Say whether our country might still have the strength
to hear of the deeds that we have to tell;
say whether the words we'll be using to bring
tears to her eyes are living, or have died.

30   And if the memory of other deeds lives on,
if the marching peaks that make us all strong
still rise and show serene above the storm
and their forests still wail in the west wind,
then brothers and sisters, waiting in grief along the shore,
35   dry your tears: let go a laugh and break out in song!

FROM SCATTERINGS
(*LES DISPERSES*, 1904)

From December 1903 to March 1904 the weekly magazine *Joventut* published a literary supplement featuring the serial appearance of poems under the title *Les disperses*, to come out in a single volume later that year, twenty of which were composed by Maragall between 1881 and 1903, followed by a second part with some thirty poems by Goethe translated into Catalan by Maragall; the only among Maragall's five volumes of poetry published by Biblioteca Joventut (the other four were brought out by L'Avenç), it was the only one not paid for by Maragall himself (see Casals 1998, 403-405; Abrams 2010, 227). Long the brunt of criticism for its limited success, the volume has been shunned for an alleged lack of thematic unity and for being "padded" with the Goethe translations tacked onto it; separately, Casals (413-414) points out how 1904 was a particularly prolific year for the Catalan-language publishing of both Catalan writers and works in Catalan translation, making for a field of sharp literary rivalry that undermined the book's chances for success. Still, in a more recent uncanonic reading of the volume, Abrams sets out swimming against the critical current: "It seems I have the honor of being the first person to weigh in seriously in favor" (2010, 228).

Abrams goes on:

In *Les disperses* Maragall went about applying to himself, exclusively, the richness and complexity of human identity [coming into] view. He knew that his own personhood was not one-dimensional, that it was plural and contradictory, that it had developed over the course of years. [...] *Les disperses* is a sort of existential inventory of Maragall's varying personalities taken on during the various stages of his life. (229-230)

The very title conveys two distinct meanings: the plurality of life's "stages during which he wrote the poems" and "the different I's throughout his life" (230). Casals, too, sees thematic consistency in the volume:

The poems selected are precisely those that interweave most clearly with those published in *Poesies* and [the] *Intermezzo* [section of *Visions & Cants*], as if Maragall sought to develop his central themes to the full: love, landscape, the passage of time, etc. (1998, 410)

As for the Goethe translations, Abrams argues that far from being added as padding to the volume, these "complete [Maragall's] examination of his personality as manifested through projection across the work of another" (2010, 231).

In his preface dedicated to the publisher, "Als amics de *Joventut*," Maragall makes it clear that he is aware of the risky nature of anthologizing too loosely, and that he feels drawn by "the temptation to assemble all those [poems] that had not fit into the unity I wished to achieve in my previous volumes" (Maragall [1904b] 2010, 109). Admitting his own "childish" indulgence in wanting "to see myself published over such a wide span of years," Maragall then tacks into the wind of his own self-criticism, declaring "a certain faith in childishness," which is "the most beautiful thing in life," and that in what "appears to be foolishness, there is perhaps a hidden transcendence of the very depths of our being" (110).

This transcendence posited in things childish comes through remarkably in the short poem "Jugant" ("At Play"); composed in 1884, it predates almost all the other poems in the volume. Abrams underscores Maragall's subtle sense of playfulness and humor: "through the poem, Maragall is playing with his readers, too, providing that they catch on" (2010, 236-237). Both Casals (1998, 430-431) and Abrams (237) point out the poem's intertextual resonance with Heinrich Heine (1797-1856), whom the young Maragall admired (Moreta 2010, 44), and whose *Lyrisches Intermezzo* precedes Maragall's playful approach to sexual awakening (see endnotes to lines 1-3 and 7-11).

"Hospitalàries" ("Hospitalities") exemplifies Maragall's awe and respect for the speech and lore of those who live close to the land—a notion he elaborated on at length in his *Elogi de la paraula* (In Praise of Words), written the same year as this poem. The poem tells of a herdsman from the Montseny mountains with whom Maragall and his good friend Josep Pijoan (1881-1963) became acquainted:

[…] an aging herdsman who was blind from cataracts, but could still make out [the disk of] the sun and followed his herd by rote. We ended up bringing him to Santa Creu Hospital in Barcelona for treatment, and there we paid him visits, and he paid us [with his] songs. Maragall recounts one of those visits in his poem "Hospitalàries." The poor cowherd that day sadly recited a sweet-tuned song whose refrain was "Fetched in the morning / they glow the whole day through." (Pijoan 2010, 77)

The poem's title conveys, in Catalan, the ambivalence of the adjective "hospitalàries," evoking both "hospital" and "hospitality," and referring here to the noun—implicit, but absent from the herdsman's song—"flowers." Abrams has noted how the herdsman's grief at being far from his mountain home interlocks with the purpose of art—represented here by both the herdsman's song and Maragall's poem—which is to enable "humanity to struggle against the annihilation entailed in death and destruction" (2010, 261).

For all its disarming simplicity, the parable-like "Soleiada" ("Sunstruck") challenges the morality of social stigma associated with single-mother pregnancy—in stark contrast to the pattern of social rejection and (self-)destruction so powerfully depicted in the dramatic monologue *La infanticida* (*The Infanticide*) by Caterina Albert (aka Víctor Català, 1869-1966), which won the Jocs Florals in Olot in 1898 (English translation by Kathleen McNerney, 2018). While avoiding specific religious reference, the poem's use of archetypical imagery makes it a striking example of what Ricard Torrents has called "de-dogmatizing":

To de-dogmatize means to mythicize. To leave the dogmatic paradigm and embrace the mythic. In perceiving the myth's content, which compels us to dream, and leave behind the dogmatic content, which compels obedience [...] art unites, dogma divides. (2006, 56)

The strength of Maragall's poem lies largely in its simplicity and frankness of statement, celebrating the joy and mystery of biological, worldly life, and shunning, at the same time, any hint of guilt or sin in connection with human reproduction. In his extraordinary verse commentary of the poem, Enric Casasses (2014) serves up a thoroughgoing inquiry into the mystery and force of its simplicity (see endnotes to this poem).

"Les roses franques" ("Non-Taxable Roses") brings the first part of *Les disperses* to a remarkable close. The last of the twenty original Maragall poems in the volume (followed by his Goethe translations), it first appeared in Maragall's sixth letter (4 May 1903) to Caterina Albert, who had revealed to him only a few months earlier Víctor Català's true identity (see Muñoz i Pairet 2015, 44). Likening Albert to the non-taxable roses, Maragall admired "the beautiful independence of her person above the artist's work and public;" conversely, Maragall reveals to her his relief at having recently freed himself of the obligation to write regular contributions to *Diario de Barcelona*, the cause, he confides, of a growing feeling of "emptiness and insincerity" (Maragall [1903a] 1960, 943). Albert, in turn, praised Maragall as "the freest and most independent of Catalonia's poets [...] the most modern and cosmopolitan of them all." Albert elaborated on how Maragall's poems stood in contrast to those of other poets, who were:

Sculptural, yes, sculptural, after the fashion of Michelangelo and Bernini, masters of things material, translators of visions from visible life; you, on the other hand, are a modeler of visions from the life [that is] invisible, of secret and fleeting states of the soul, of delicate and refined emotions; your poems [combine] the strange vagueness and the strange precision of modern medals, with fluctuating lines, graceful curves and irregularities of a penetrating and unspecifiable beauty, distinct from any and all codified beauty. (Albert 1903)

This poem, like "La vaca cega," is an outstanding example of Maragall's working "with the noble raw material provided for him by immediate reality" (Abrams 2010, 71) and translating the sensations brought about by that reality directly into poetry. In the letter to Albert cited above, Maragall tells about "expressing the impression of some flowers growing above a wall in one of the many neighborhood gardens […] near where I live" (Maragall [1903a] 1960, 942). Quintana (2008, 11) notes how "in the city nothing is wild, everything has been created by man, who seeks to control it all," but these roses " 'belong to the wind and the sun,' eluding the owners of the gardens, […] mocking them, as they 'sway and laugh,'" and when their life cycle draws to a close, "it is not the sad death of [other] roses, whose petals fall on the table until we grow tired of them and toss them out"— these roses, in contrast, "return to their origins." All in all, concludes Abrams, "Non-Taxable Roses" is a "proud poem about human freedom, the generous universality of art and beauty, interaction in the world without servitude, the importance of alert awareness, and the carrying out of the life cycle to the full" (2010, 300; see endnotes to this poem).

JUGANT

«Campaneta, la ning-ning,
qui la troba?, no la tinc.»
«Quina és la prenda amagada?»
«Una ànima enamorada.»
5   Va acudir un eixam de noies
eixerides, alegroies,
com les mosques a la mel.
«On és, per cel o per terra?»
Jo els ulls mirant amb fal·lera
10 d'una, la més encisera,
vaig dir mig rient:
            «Pel cel.»

AT PLAY

"Tiny bell, ring-a-ling,
Who can find it? Haven't got it."
"What is this thing that's a-hiding?"
"A soul in love."
5   Along came a swarm of girls,
vivacious, all a-swirls,
like houseflies to honey.
"Where is it? Heaven or earth?"
And looking with relish into the eyes
10 of one, the most delightful,
I said with a grin,
                  " 'N heaven."

HOSPITALÀRIES

«Collides al dematí,
tot lo dia són rosades.»
En aquell Sant Hospital
el pastor vell de muntanya
5   embenat i llatzerat,
lluny de la muntanya amada,
entre aquells murs de dolor
i aquella mala bravada,
sota el sostre tenebrós
10   tan different d'aquell altre,
tornava de tant en tant
que barrejava paraules:
«Collides al dematí,
tot lo dia són rosades.»

15   Embarbussava cançons
ja sense el goig de cantar-les;
només deia sens parar
en l'anguniosa estada,
deia, deia… jo no ho sé,
20   per mi tot gemecs i basques,
pro només de tant en tant
aquella fresca tornada:
«Collides al dematí,
tot lo dia són rosades.»
25   Devia parlar de flors
segons jo en sentia flaire.

HOSPITALITIES

"Fetched in the morning,
they glow the whole day through."
There in the saintly hospital,
the old mountain herder
5   bandaged and swollen,
far from the mountain he loved,
within these sorry walls,
amid the stench,
beneath a dismal roof
10   so different from that other,
it happened, now and then,
would mutter these words:
"Fetched in the morning,
they glow the whole day through."

15   He'd garble out songs,
the pleasure of singing gone,
went on and on
the length of his bleak stay,
uttering, uttering… what, I don't know,
20   all groans and anguish to me,
but then from time to time
that bright refrain anew:
"Fetched in the morning,
they glow the whole day through."
25   From what I could gather,
he must have been talking of flowers.

SOLEIADA

En una casa de pagès hi havia
una donzella que tenia
els disset anys d'amor; i era tan bella,
que la gent d'aquell volt
5 deien: «És una noia com un sol.»
Ella prou la sabia
la parentela que amb el sol tenia:
que cada matinada
per la finestra a sol ixent badada,
10 l'astre de foc i ambre
li entrava de ple a ple dintre la cambra,
i ella nua, amb delícia,
s'abandonava a la fulgent carícia.
De tant donar-se a aquestes dolces manyes
15 va ficar-se-li el sol a les entranyes,
i ben prompte sentia
una ardència dins d'ella que es movia.
«Adéu, la casa meva i els que hi són:
jo prenyada de llum me'n vaig pel món.»
20 De tots abandonada,
va començar a rodar per l'encontrada.
Estava alegre com l'aucell que vola,
cantava tota sola,
cantava: «Só l'albada
25 que duc el sol a dins i en só rosada.
Els cabells me rossegen,
els ulls me guspiregen,

SUNSTRUCK

There lived in a house in the country
a girl of seventeen summers
of love, and so lovely she was
that people from all around
5   said: "That girl is like sunshine."
She herself was not unaware
of the kinship she shared with the sun:
each morning through her window,
opening wide to the eastern sky,
10 that fire-and-amber sphere
came streaming through her room,
and she, disrobed, would give herself
with relish to its radiant caress.
So taken was she with its touch
15 that the sun took a spot within her,
and soon she felt
a spark that stirred inside her.
"Good-bye my home and kin:
I, laden with light, set out to walk the world."
20 Abandoned by everyone, off
she went to roam the countryside,
glad as a bird in the sky,
with a song she sang all alone:
"I am the breaking day,
25 tinged with rose from the sun I hold inside.
My hair shines,
my eyes sparkle,

els llavis me robiegen,
en les galtes i el front tinc el color
30 i al pit la gran cremor:
tota jo só claror contra claror.»
La gent que la sentia
s'aturava admirada i la seguia:
la seguia pel pla i per la muntanya
35 per sentir-li cantar la cançó estranya
que l'anava embellint de mica en mica.
Quan ella va sentir-se prou bonica,
va dir: «M'ha arribat l'hora»,
va parar de cantar, i allà a la vora
40 entrava a una barraca que hi havia.
La gent que a l'entorn era
sols veia un resplendor i sols sentia
el gemec poderós de la partera.
De sobte, les clivelles
45 del tancat van lluir igual que estrelles.
De seguit s'aixecà gran foguerada,
tota la gent fugia esparverada,
i en la gran soletat només restava
un nin igual que el sol, que caminava
50 i deia tot pujant amunt la serra:
«Jo vinc per acostar el cel a la terra...»

my lips redden like rubies,
I feel the flush in my cheeks and forehead,
30   and the great burning in my breast:
all of me is light against light."
People who heard her
stopped in surprise and followed:
over plains and up mountains they followed,
35   eager to hear the strange song,
which she embellished as she went along.
Then, feeling that she was lovely enough,
she said: "It's time."
She stopped her singing, and walked into
40   a hut that stood along the way.
The people all around
saw only a bright light, and heard
only the mother's birth cries.
Suddenly, the cracks in the hut
45   dazzled with the strength of stars.
Then a great blaze burst out,
everyone ran off in fright,
and in the empty solitude there stood but
a child, identical to the sun, and who took to
50   the summits and spoke these words:
"I come to bring the heavens nearer the earth…"

LES ROSES FRANQUES

He vist unes roses — d'un vermell pujat,
d'un vermell negrós, — d'un vermell morat.
Penjaven gronxant-se — del mur d'un jardí:
ningú les pot heure, — ne es poden collir.
5   Són les roses lliures — de la servitud,
són les roses franques, —no paguen tribut.
Ni de baix s'abasten — ni de dalt estant:
el gipó ni el gerro — no se'n gaudiran.
Brillar al sol veuran-les — des de lluny la gent,
10   donaran la flaire — al bon grat del vent;
mes cap mà atrevida — les apomarà
ni alenada humana — les mustigarà.
No com les flors altres, — són de qui les vol:
són lliures, són pures, — són del vent i el sol.
15   Passaran la vida — gronxant-se i rient,
i abrusades se les emportarà el vent.

NON-TAXABLE ROSES

I saw some roses, bright red ones,
some dark red ones, some purply-red ones.
They swayed high on a garden wall:
no one could reach them, they couldn't be picked.
5   These roses know no servitude,
they are non-taxable, no duty attached.
They can't be had from down below, or up above:
no vase or lapel will display them.
They shine in the sun and are seen from a distance,
10   their fragrance delivered: courtesy of the breeze;
no brazen hand will bouquet them,
no human breath will taint them.
Not like other flowers, they're anyone's:
they're free and pure, and belong to the wind and the sun.
15   They'll sway and laugh their days away,
and once dried up, they'll be fetched by the wind.

FROM BEYOND
(*ENLLÀ*, 1906)

Published in May 1906, *Enllà* met with a sharply polarized reception amid a particularly heated literary and cultural context (see Casals 1998, 589-604; Abrams 2010, 311-317). To begin with, the year 1906 ushered in such landmark events in Catalonia's cultural and political history as the first Congrés Internacional de la Llengua Catalana and the Solidaritat Catalana movement, which under Enric Prat de la Riba (1870-1917), rallied together a wide range of Catalan political parties against the encroachment of Spanish military authority in civilian life in the form of the Ley de Jurisdicciones, a law which broadened the scope of military tribunals; Prat de la Riba's seminal essay *La nacionalitat catalana* appeared this same year. In Catalan poetry, the remarkable year 1906 saw, along with Maragall's *Enllà*, the appearance of long-enduring works by Mallorcan poet-priest Miquel Costa i Llobera (1854-1922) and Barcelona-born Josep Carner (1884-1970), hailed as harbingers of the literary and cultural movement known as Noucentisme, whose outspoken advocate Eugeni d'Ors (1881-1954) depicted the movement as a fitting cultural and political antidote against Modernisme and its most prominent poet—Maragall. On the aesthetic turning from Modernisme to Noucentisme Arthur Terry observes:

The division between centuries is never clear-cut: in Catalonia, Modernisme retained its force at least until 1911, the year which saw the death of Maragall […] In the meantime, however, a new movement had come to the fore—Noucentisme—which made its presence felt a few years earlier, in 1906. Before this, even the most original writers were related in one way or another to [the nineteenth-century Romantics of] the Renaixença, though some of them, like Maragall, were directly concerned with the political and social events of the time. (Terry 2003, 84)

The all-out critical attack on Maragall in 1906 by the emerging Noucentista movement, which defined itself largely on its rejection of Modernisme, ratcheted up the tensions on both sides of the new book's critical reception:

On one hand, it drew praise from Maragall's steadfast adherents; on the other hand, it drew open fire from the group of Noucentistes commandeered by Eugeni d'Ors. Probably, had it not been for the blind devotion of the former and the high-handed onslaught of the latter, there would have been some agreement about the intrinsic merits of the book. This is what would have happened if the book had come out a few years earlier, or later, when neither the assault of the Noucentistes to gain ground nor the final struggle of the Modernistes to hold their own were expressed in such inflexible terms. (Casals 1998, 596)

Be as it may, the first edition's five hundred copies all sold and the volume earned itself solid recognition four years later when it was awarded the prestigious Fastenrath Prize in 1910 for the "best book of poetry in Catalan published during the last six years," competing against, among others, Costa i Llobera's *Horacianes*, published also in the signal year 1906 (591, 603).

As for the volume's title (which, it turns out, is not what Maragall had in mind at first; see Casals 1998, 590), Abrams (2010, 314) identifies four levels on which *Enllà* (Beyond) might be understood: first, going "beyond the surface of objects and events;" second, realizing the human potential to "construct meanings that are more or less stable based on the fragmented and intermittent experience [...] of the senses and the mind;" third, underscoring "the capacity of the human mind to go beyond the physical limits of life in its quest for overall knowledge;" and fourth, "the ability of poets to go beyond the limits of their texts [...] and theorize on the art of poetry." We need only recall the poem "Excelsior"—epilogue to Maragall's first volume of poetry (see headnote to *Poesies*), where he lays the groundwork for the poet's going beyond—to appreciate how Maragall's quest gains in breadth and depth throughout his life's work. In a word, as Casals remarks, this title is "the most Maragallian of them all" (591).

Brilliant in its apparent simplicity, the short series poem "Vistes al mar" ("Views of the Sea") and its sequel "Seguit de les vistes al mar" inspired composer Eduard Toldrà's (1895-1962) widely performed string quartet *Vistes al mar* (1920, later arranged for chamber orchestra). Written by Maragall in stages during a family sojourn in the spring of 1901 at the seaside resort town of Caldes d'Estrac (known as "Caldetes"), the poem soon appeared in the magazine *Joventut* and was dedicated to Víctor Català (Maragall did not yet know her real name or identity; see headnote to *Les disperses*), who had recently dedicated to Maragall her poem "L'oca blanca" which appeared in March, also in *Joventut* (see Casals 1998, 609-615). In "Vistes al mar" Maragall turns his attention once again to the seascape—for the first time, Casals (610) reminds us, since his 1891 visit with his fiancée's family near Bilbao. In contrast, however, to the earlier poetic re-creation of the seascape as an "objective correlate for expressing the effervescent joy" felt by the young man soon to be married (610), now the internalization and poetic re-creation of the seascape broadens in scope, brushing the threshold of what Abrams observes are, in connection with the poem, "the two levels of reality, the immediate and the transcendent" (2010, 329). The magnitude of Maragall's epistemic query and its potent imagery and lyricism are all the more striking for the poem's simplicity of lexis and structure. In his fifth and final volume of poetry, *Seqüències* (1911), Maragall will again take up the seascape motif in "Seguit de les vistes al mar" (Continuing Views of the Sea; not included in this selection).

After their seaside holiday in Caldes d'Estrac, Maragall and his family sojourned in the Pyrenean town of Camprodon, some ten miles northeast of Sant Joan de les Abadesses (see notes to "The Cow Gone Blind"), where he composed the powerfully lyrical poem "Les muntanyes" ("The Mountains"), in which the springwater fountain of Sant Patllari serves as catalyst for the poet's extraordinary en-counter with "the secrets / of the mysterious earth." The outcome of the poetized encounter is, as Terry has put it, direct access to a "telluric wisdom" (1999, 100) stemming from a moment of terrestrial communion engaging both the senses and the mind of the poet, and recalling not pantheism but rather "pananthropism" (Serrahima 1981, 106), in which it is the human spirit, rather than the divine, that coalesces with the natural world.

With the extraordinary series poem "Retorn" ("Return"), Maragall returns to the mountains as the point of departure for his poetic inquiry; yet more particularly, and given the temporal and physical proximity in the composition of "Les muntanyes" and "Retorn," we may glean also from the title a return to the self once again separate from the natural world, whereupon the human spirit now confronts, or engages, the world rather than fusing or coalescing with it. In the first three of the poem's five sections, the compelling but impenetrable essence of the mountains imposes the realization that the "freedom of the peaks" remains elusive (section I), realization which then leads to sadness (section II), and finally brings on a sense of dread, triggering the poet's flight to the flatlands (section III). In sharp contrast to the unassailable essence of the mountains, the institutionalized spiritualism en masse depicted in bold strokes by Maragall at Lourdes (section IV) evokes a sense of unfreedom ("human flocks / bleating their grand bleat") and senseless suffering ("the terrible column / of the stricken"). Still, the vision of the "miracle, which blossoms gently / among the reddish rays of the lowering sun," also retains, as do the mountains, an aura of beauty and wonder. In the concluding fifth section of the poem, it is a historical vision of the once glorious land of Béarn ("Hail, noble Béarn! Land of liberty") that evokes a longing for a freedom no less elusive and compelling than the mountains themselves, the returning but elusive vision of which closes the poem—now lifted from the present and projected into winter.

With the turning of seasons, it is from this winter—now become present—that the vision of the mountains is revisited from afar, glimpsed from the distant city ("from the summits of my Barcelona"), reactivating and revitalizing the force of the previous summer's poetic inquiry: the anticipated "winter, beneath the sun all white with snow" (closing the previous poem, "Return") now opens the short poem "Retake," expanding and completing the inquiry in what Abrams has called a masterful colophon to "Return" (2010, 360), reaffirming the power of poetry in challenging the limits of self in time and space, and coming full circle in taking up again the very imagery opening the volume's first two poems: "The Almond Trees" (not included in this selection) and "Views of the Sea."

The penning of *El comte Arnau* (part two), sparked anew by Maragall's creative encounter with Count Arnau—the morally conflictive figure looming large in popular Catalan legend (see headnote to *Visions & Cants*)—gained further traction from composer Felip Pedrell (1841-1922), who undertook the project of putting Maragall's text to music as the second part of the poem took shape between 1901 and 1904. The poet's progress, however, was slowgoing:

[…] From time to time the characters appear to me, they speak, and I listen to them, and I write down what they say, and then they're gone, and I don't think about them any more till they return again at some unlikely hour—and so on; more than this I cannot do. Will they return tomorrow? Today? Ever again? I cannot say. (letter from Maragall to Pedrell, 1903c)

Where Pedrell was concerned, pressure to step up the project's pace was compounded by the imminent appearance of a separately staged *Comte Arnau* by Noucentista writer Josep Carner (1884-1970), with musical accompaniment by renowned composer Enric Morera (1865-1942). Pedrell met the challenge and completed the work in hopes of a June 1904 premiere, but the composer's grandiose scheme to stage a one-event festival–production at Park Güell (or alternatively, Barcelona's bullring) for an audience of thousands fell short on sponsorship; meanwhile, the Carner–Morera tandem's *Comte Arnau*, hailed by critics, opened at the Teatre Principal on 14 October 1905 (see Casals 1998, 671-682; Radigales 1997, 19-30). Included in this selection is part two's closing section, titled "Scholium" (see endnotes).

VISTES AL MAR

DE LA NIT PER LO PREGON,
ENTRE CANTS I LLUM ESTRANYA,
BAIXAVEN DE LA MUNTANYA
AL DOLOR COM REI DEL MÓN

NIT DEL DIVENDRES SANT
CALDETES, 4-IV-1901

I

Vora la mar eternament inquieta
floreix immòbil la pomera blanca,
i el presseguer vermell, que riu i brilla
prop la mar inquieta aquietadora.

II

5   Degué ser un dia així que el bon Jesús
caminà sobre el mar; el cel i l'aigua
serien, com avui, llisos i blaus...
I la Visió anà ràpida a l'encontre
dels encantats deixebles en la barca.

III

10   El cel ben serè
torna el mar més blau,
d'un blau que enamora
al migdia clar:
entre els pins me'l miro...
15   Dues coses hi ha
que el mirar-les juntes

VIEWS OF THE SEA

IN THE VERY DEEP OF NIGHT,
IN SONG AND BY STRANGE LIGHT,
DOWN THE MOUNTAIN THEY LOWERED
SORROW, AS KING OF THE WORLD.

THE NIGHT OF GOOD FRIDAY
CALDES D'ESTRAC, 4 APRIL 1901

I

Beside the sea forever restless
blossoms, not budging, a white apple tree,
and a red peach tree sparkling and shining
close by the restful, restless sea.

II

5   Must've been a day like this the Good Lord
walked the sea: the sky and water
would have shone, like today, smooth and blue…
And the Vision strode along to meet
the astounded disciples out in the boat.

III

10   The sky all serene
turns the sea the more blue,
a blue that delights
in the clear noon:
I look through the pine trees…
15   There are two things here
that joined into view

me fa el cor més gran:
la verdor dels pins,
la blavor del mar.

IV

20   El vent se desferma
i tot el mar canta.
Mar brava, mar verda, mar escumejanta!
L'onada s'adreça;
venint s'ageganta,
25   avença i s'acosta
callada que espanta.
L'escuma enlluerna,
el sol l'abrillanta,
l'onada s'esberla
30   i cau ressonanta.
Mar brava, mar verda, mar escumejanta!

V

Una a una, com verges a la dansa,
entren lliscant les barques en el mar;
s'obre la vela com una ala al sol,
35   i per camins que només elles veuen
s'allunyen mar endintre...
Oh cel blau! Oh mar blau, platja deserta,
groga de sol! De prop el mar te canta,
mentres tu esperes el retorn magnífic,
40   a sol ponent, de la primera barca,
que sortirà del mar tota olorosa.

make my heart grow wide:
the green of the pines,
the blue of the sea.

IV

20   The winds are rising
and the whole sea sings.
Sea rolling, sea green, sea foaming!
    A wave rears up
    gathering and growing,
25   advancing and nearing
    frightful in its silence.
    The foam dazzles,
    the sun strikes it,
    the wave breaks
30   and falls with a crash.
Sea rolling, sea green, sea foaming!

V

One by one, like maidens in dance,
the boats slide into the sea,
each sail like a wing spread in the sun,
35   and tracing pathways seen only by them
        they make their way out to sea…
Blue skies! Blue sea, empty beach,
yellow from sun! Close by, the sea sings to you,
while you await the magnificent return,
40   at sunset, of that first boat:
come out from the sea all fragrant.

LES MUNTANYES

A l'hora que el sol se pon,
bevent al raig de la font,
he assaborit els secrets
de la terra misteriosa.

5   Part de dins de la canal
he vist l'aigua virginal
venir del fosc naixement
a regalar-me la boca,

   i m'entrava pit endins…
10   I amb els seus clars regalims
penetrava-m'hi ensems
una saviesa dolça.

   Quan m'he adreçat i he mirat,
la muntanya, el bosc i el prat
15   me semblaven altrament:
tot semblava una altra cosa.

   Al damunt del bell morir
començava a resplendir
pels celatges carminencs
20   el blanc quart de lluna nova.

   Tot semblava un món en flor
i l'ànima n'era jo.

   Jo l'ànima flairosa de la prada
que es delita en florir i en ser dallada.

THE MOUNTAINS

The hour the sun goes down,
as I drank from the trickling fount,
I took in a taste of the secrets
of the mysterious earth.

5   Inside the gorge, up farther,
I saw the virginal waters
coming out from their deep
birth, to slake my thirst,

and they entered inside my chest…
10   And along with the clear jet
there penetrated, too, within me
a wisdom that reassured.

When then, I straightened up to look,
the mountain, pasture and wood
15   looked different to me: they all seemed
something other than they were.

Above the beautiful dying
in carmine-colored skies
there now began to gleam
20   a moon in its first quarter.

It all seemed a world in bloom
and I was its soul.

I, the scented soul of fields
in delectable flowering and reaping.

25 Jo l'ànima pacífica del ramat
    esquellejant pel bac mig amagat.

    Jo l'ànima del bosc que fa remor
    com el mar, que és tan lluny en l'horitzó.

    I l'ànima del saule jo era encara
30 que dóna a tota font son ombra clara.

    Jo de la timba l'ànima profonda
    on la boira s'aixeca i es deixonda.

    Jo l'ànima inquieta del torrent
    que crida en la cascata resplendent.

35 Jo era l'ànima blava de l'estany
    que aguaita el viatger amb ull estrany.

    Jo l'ànima del vent que tot ho mou
    i la humil de la flor quan se desclou.

    Jo era l'altitud de la carena…

40 Els núvols m'estimaven llargament,
    i al llarg amor de l'ennuvolament
    congriava's mon ànima serena.

    Sentia la delícia de les fonts
    nàixer en mon si, regal de les congestes;
45 i en l'ampla quietud dels horitzons
    hi sentia el repòs de les tempestes.

    I quan el cel s'obria al meu entorn
    i reia el sol en ma verdosa plana,
    les gents, al lluny, restaven tot el jorn

25 I, the peaceful soul of flocks,
bells clunking half-hidden in hollows.

  I, the soul of woods whose murmurs rise
like the sea far out on the horizon.

  And the soul of willows that grace
30 their every fount with clear shade.

  I, the deep-flung soul of cliffs
where fog will float and lift.

  And of mountain streams the restless soul
crying out in gleaming waterfalls.

35 I was the blue soul of lakes
that eye the traveler strangely.

  I, the soul of the wind that moves all,
and of budding flowers, humble soul.

  I was the heights of ranging peaks…

40 Clouds loved me long, and from
the clouds, and their long love,
there settled in my soul a serenity.

  I felt the delight of wellsprings,
gift of snowdrifts, surging in my core;
45 and on the horizon's broad calm
I felt the repose of storms.

  And when the sky opened up all around me
and the sun sparkled down on my green plains,
the people, far off, stood long through the day

50   contemplant ma bellesa sobirana.

Però jo, tota plena de l'anhel
agitador del mar i les muntanyes,
fortament m'adreçava per dur al cel
tot lo de mos costats i mes entranyes.

....

55   A l'hora que el sol se pon,
bevent al raig de la font,
he assaborit els secrets
de la terra misteriosa.

50   and gazed at my sovereign loveliness.

      But I, replete with the desire
      that stirs in the mountains and seas,
      stood sturdily up to carry to the skies
      all that was around me and within me.

. . . .

55   The hour the sun goes down,
      as I drank from the trickling fount,
      I took in a taste of the secrets
      of the mysterious earth.

RETORN

I

Oh Pirineu! En tes profondes gorges,
fill de la plana, m'he sentit com pres,
i amb l'esguard demanava al cel altíssim
    amplària i vent.
5 Pujava per tes costes gegantines
    on blanquegen les cascades
    i negregen els avets;
    on la flor de la muntanya
perfumava el meu gran enyorament…
10 La llibertat dels cims no l'assolia:
    restava a vora d'ells.

II

En alta solitud s'està pels sigles
    el blau estany immòbil,
mirant-se al Vignemale, que li mostra
15   sa faldada de neu:
jo a l'hora del capvespre hi arribava
    i a prop de l'aigua quieta
    m'asseia tristament.

III

Cercava Gavarnie entre les boires
20   on llisquen les cascades
al llarg del mur immens pausadament;

RETURN

I

Pyrenees! In your deep ravines,
son of flatlands, I've felt captive,
my eyes asking the high skies
    for broadness and wind.
5 I've climbed your gigantic sides
    where cascades plunge white
    and fir trees stretch black;
    where mountain flowers
fragranced my heartfelt longing…
10 The freedom of the peaks, I never found:
    I only approached them.

II

In high solitude there lies through the centuries
    a lake, blue and unmoving,
watching Vignemale, who displays
15   her snow-filled lap:
it was late afternoon when I got there
    and sadly sat
    by the still waters.

III

I searched through the mist for Gavarnie
20   where the cascades glide
by degrees down the huge walls;

i al ser-hi he sospirat per trobar aire
i he hagut d'aixecar el cap per veure el cel.

I, trencant ton encís d'una vegada,
25   oh Pirineu terrible!
    a la plana de Tarbes
    me n'he baixat corrents.

IV

An els teus peus, a ratlla de la plana,
Lourdes devota té molt bell el cel:
30   el sol hi daura la ramada humana
      que bela amb un gran bel
      davant la Verge blanca,
      davant la iglésia freda;
    i enmig del baf de les gentades tèrboles
35   s'alça el miracle i dolçament floreix
    als vermellosos raigs del sol ponent…

    (Passar jo l'he vista — l'horrible filera
dels malalts en braços dels homes de fe:
les boques inflades, — les conques morades,
40   el cos sense gest.
I aquella malalta — tan blanca, tan rossa,
no me la puc treure mai del pensament.
Sols ella mig reia. Jo crec que era morta.)

    Al vespre un riu de llumenetes grogues
45   passa en la fosca ressonant de veus.

and once there, I gasped for air
and had to lift my head to see the sky.

Then, breaking from your spell at last,
25   dreaded Pyrenees!
      I sped my way down
      to the plains of Tarbes.

IV

At your feet, at the flatlands' edge,
holy Lourdes shows a lovely sky:
30   the sunlight gilds her human flocks
      bleating their grand bleat
      before the White Virgin,
      before the cold church;
and above the reek of the muddling crowd
35   there lifts the miracle, which blossoms gently
among the reddish rays of the lowering sun…

  (I saw, as it passed, the terrible column
of the stricken conveyed in the arms of men of faith:
mouths swollen, sockets purpled,
40   bodies sans movement.
And that one sick girl, so pale, so pretty,
I'll never shake her from my mind.
Half-smiling, only she. I believe she was dead.)

  In the evening a river of points, yellow lights,
45 passing in the darkness that echoes with voices.

V

Salut, noble Bearn! Oh terra franca.
  mare de cavallers
que es jugaven la vida a cops d'espasa
  bravejant i rient!
50 Abocat a l'airosa balconada
jo t'he cantat de lluny, oh Pirineu!
veient tos cims com rengle de fantasmes
vestits de llum en la blavor del cel.
  Adéu, visió darrera
55   de l'alta cordillera!
Que en deus estar d'hermosa,
a l'hivern, sota el sol blanca de neu!

V

Hail, noble Béarn! Land of liberty,
    mother to musketeers
who risked their skins crossing swords
    with gusto and laughter!
50 Leaning out on the graceful balcony
I've sung you from afar, Pyrenees!
Seeing your summits like a row of ghosts
garbed in light against the sky's blue.
    Good-bye, last vision
55   of your tall cordillera!
How lovely you must be
in winter, under the sun all white with snow!

REPRESA

A l'hivern, sota el sol blanca de neu,
com visió més llunyana i més formosa,
jo t'he vist resplendir en l'aire clar
des dels cims de la meva Barcelona,
5   on tots els ametllers ja són florits
davant del mar brillant fins a Mallorca.

RETAKE

In winter, under the sun all white with snow:
a vision, now further off and lovelier,
I've seen you glimmering in the clear air
from the summits of my Barcelona,
5   where all the almond trees have blossomed
before the sea that gleams out to Mallorca.

FROM EL COMTE ARNAU
(SEGONA PART: L'ÀNIMA)

ESCOLIUM

Com dos que enraonant van de costat
tot caminant per un camí partit,
l'un pel caire del marge assoleiat,
455 i l'altre a baix pel bac tot ensombrit,
Adalaisa i el poeta s'han parlat,
cos i esprit ell, mes ella tota esprit.

ADALAISA

Ai! Quina angúnia aquest camí!
Tan fosc, tan fosc, i tan de mal seguir!
460 Vegés almenys el sol i les muntanyes,
les coses resplendint sota el cel blau,
i no pas aquest llim de veus estranyes
sense forma ni color… Digues, Arnau:
qui és aquest que per la trista via
465 nos va menant com ombres sens virtut?
Prou serà algun poeta que somnia
el somni de l'eterna inquietud.

EL POETA

Vius la vida veritable
de l'esprit, i encara et dol?
470 Camines a lo immutable…

FROM COUNT ARNAU
(PART TWO: THE SOUL)

SCHOLIUM

As two conversing one beside the other
While walking a path that runs divided,
One along the sunny stretch above,
455 The other, below, on the shadowy side,
Adalaisa and the poet now speak:
Body and spirit he, all spirit she.

ADALAISA

Ugh! This path gives me the creeps!
It's so dark, and hard to keep on the track!
460 If I at least could see the sun and hills,
And all that's bright beneath blue skies,
Instead of this muck-lode of odd voices,
shapeless and colorless… Say, Arnau:
Who's that there on the drab path now
465 Leading us like shadows lacking virtue?
Likely some poet who's dreaming
The dream of eternal restlessness.

POET

You live the true life
Of the spirit, and still you suffer?
470 You walk toward the immutable…

ADALAISA

No hi ha res com veure el sol!
Doncs tu treu-nos a la via
de les coses corporals,
bon amic, baldament sia
475 per patir-hi tots els mals.
Mal la llum ens enlluerni,
mal el so ens deixi atuïts,
mal el cos tot se'ns inferni,
patint amb tots els sentits,
480 jo vull la vida primera,
veure, oir, gustar, tocar:
jo no en sé d'altra manera,
ni cap altra en vull provar.

EL POETA

La vida que ara tu ansies
485 és la gran resurrecció.
Prou no et fóra la que havies,
però l'altra encara no.

ADALAISA

Doncs tu bé te n'acontentes,
de la vida que ara tens.

EL POETA

490 Si jo puc veure al bell través del món
lo que per tu és un pur goig o turment,
sí que de la meva vida estic content,

ADALAISA

There's nothing like seeing the sun!
So take us walking, good friend,
Along the path of things that are
Physically and bodily, though it mean
475 Suffering ills of all sorts.
Though the light be blinding,
And the sound deafening,
And the body broken
And suffering in all its senses,
480 I want the life that came before:
to see, to hear, to taste, to touch—
I know no other,
No other care to try.

POET

The life that you now long for
485 Is the great resurrection.
The life you had would fall short,
And the other is yet to come.

ADALAISA

You sure seem satisfied
With your present life.

POET

490 If I can see in the workings of this world
What is pleasure or is pain for you,
Then yes, I'm satisfied with my life,

perquè dins d'ella dues vides són.

Mes si aquest esser fos descompartit

495 i mos sentits restessin corporals,

jo més m'estimaria abandonà'ls,

per a esser, com tu, sols un esprit.

No ara, que tot canta en mes entranyes

i que tinc muller pròpia i que tinc fills,

500 i que en el cim de les pairals muntanyes

hi ha un crit de renaixença entre perills.

De l'amor i la lluita és la meva hora

i em calen braços per aimar i lluitar.

Tot lo que tinc m'ho vull, i pit i fora…

505 Mes, què sé jo lo que voldré demà?

ADALAISA

Ditxós de tu, que pots voler amb veu viva

i que ets a temps a prendre i a deixar,

i tens a casa la muller captiva

que et dóna fills i filles a estimar.

510 Però, digues com fou que la trobares

i a on florí l'amor i a on granà;

digue'm de com les dones tornen mares

en aquest món on mai haig de tornar.

EL POETA

En una vall del Pirineu molt alta

515 un estiu la vegí per primer cop;

no la vegí sinó després molt veure-la,

perquè té la bellesa molt recòndita,

com la viola que embalsama els boscos.

Because, if so, my lives are two.
But should this being be pulled apart
495 And my senses none but bodily,
I'd just as soon be rid of them,
And be, like you, spirit only.
But not now: that all is song within me,
That I have a wife and children,
500 That from the ancestral mountaintops
Come cries of our renaissance fraught with risk.
My hour of love and struggle has come:
To struggle and to love I need my arms.
All I have I'd gladly keep—courage!
505 But how do I know what I'll want tomorrow?

ADALAISA

Lucky you—able to want in a living voice,
And not too late to take or leave,
And with a captive wife at home
Who gives you sons and daughters you can love.
510 So tell me how you came to find her
And where love bloomed and where it seeded;
Tell me what turns women into mothers
In this world where I'm never to return.

POET

High in a Pyrenean valley one summer
515 I saw her for the first time;
Long I looked before I saw:
Her beauty well concealed,
Like balmy violets deep in woods.

Mes ara jo l'he feta rosa vera
520 del meu jardí, i a més ha estat fruitosa:
perquè Déu beneïa ses entranyes
moltes voltes, i alguna doblement.
I els fruits ja no li caben a la falda,
i roden pel trespol, i són formosos.
525 Com són acostumats al bes mos llavis
i els ulls a mirar avall cap als petits,
i a doblegar-se el cos per a estimar-los
més de prop, i aixecar-los en mos braços
cap al cel, pro tenint-los ben fermats!
530 Cada bes en cad'un té el seu gust propi:
mai he besat a dos d'igual manera,
però a tots dolçament perquè són dòcils
a l'esguard maternal que a sobre els vola
amb aquell seu imperi ferm i suau.
535 Ella me'ls agombola tot el dia
i me'ls vetlla de nit, fins adormida,
oh son de mare, que vigiles més
que tot altre vetllar!… Mes, de què plores,
Adalaisa, que et sento dins la fosca?

ADALAISA

540 Ah! Tingués jo els ulls oberts a llum del dia,
d'altre crit, d'altre modo ploraria.
El xiscle esgarrifós de la partera,
com de bèstia ferida, em fóra grat;
i el fill que duc per vies tan estranyes
545 sortiria ensagnat de mes entranyes,
i jo riuria amb riure com d'orat.

But now she is my garden's
520 Crimson rose, and she's given fruit:
Many times has she been blessed by God,
And sometimes twice.
Her lap no longer holds them all,
And they romp and play, what a sight!
525 Accustomed now to kisses are my lips,
My eyes to gazing down at toddlers,
My frame to bending low to love them close
And lift them high in my arms
Toward the sky, yet hold them tight.
530 Each kiss to each possesses its own flavor:
Never have I kissed two quite the same,
Yet all sweetly, for they are gentle
Under their mother's watch that wings
Above them in firm but mild imperium.
535 She mothers them all day long
And keeps vigil nights, even sleeping,
O mother's sleep, the watch you keep
Outwatches all others!… But, why the tears,
Adalaisa, that I hear in the darkness?

ADALAISA

540 If only my eyes could see the light of day,
My cries, my crying, would be otherwise.
The mother's wail at childbirth,
Like a wounded beast's, would be to my liking;
And the child I bring on such ghostly pathways
545 Would sally forth in blood from deep inside me,
And I'd laugh the wild laugh of a madwoman.

Què em faria el dolor, ni què, el desfici,
ni tot el temps passat de sacrifici,
ni les congoixes, ni el perill de mort,
550 si de la vida me trobés com centre,
i sentís com l'infant, desprès del ventre,
morat d'ofec encara, arrenca el plor!

EL POETA

Bé la conec la vostra fortalesa
quan, regalant suor, la cara encesa,
555 solt el cabell, com astre radiant,
al sortir de la brega gloriosa,
nos doneu l'abraçada furiosa
i vostre bes ressona com un cant!
Llavores que el marit, més fred que el marbre,
560 tremola encara com la fulla a l'arbre,
dret al costat del llit tempestejat,
i ajagudes vosaltres, sens memòria,
ubriagades per la gran victòria,
el rebregueu al pit, — volent més fort combat...
565 Mes ara tu, Adalaisa, ¿què somnies
de tenir un fill, si ja no ets d'aquest món,
i en el món que ets no hi calen fills ni filles,
perquè els esprits lo que han de ser ja ho són?

ADALAISA

I, què saps tu ni d'aquest món ni d'altres
570 ni de lo que és un cos o un esperit,
ni lo que un gran desig pot en nosaltres,
restant en l'últim ai! del nostre pit?

What matter to me the pain, what matter the anguish,
What matter all the sacrifice,
The suffering, danger of death,
550 If I found myself at life's center,
And heard the infant, out from the womb
And blue without breath, let go a cry!

POET

I know of womanhood's strength
When, dripping with sweat, red-faced
555 And hair unloosed like a radiant star,
Out you come from the glorious struggle
To give us that furious embrace
And your kiss rings out like song!
The husband, struck by a chill as of marble,
560 Stands at the storm-ridden bed,
Trembling like a leaf on a tree,
While you, lying there, unmemoried,
Intoxicated by your great victory,
Press him to your breast, eager for more combat...
565 But you, Adalaisa, why this dream
Of children? You are no longer of this world,
And children play no part in your world now,
Since what spirits must be, spirits are already.

ADALAISA

And what do you know about this or other worlds,
570 Or what a body or a spirit is,
Or what a powerful desire, one final sigh,
Deep down inside us can or cannot do?

Tu em tens per morta i jo em tinc per viva;
mes tal com si enterrada viva fos,
575 tinc el voler de mos sentits furiós,
perquè hi ha alguna cosa que me'l priva.
Si no me la pots traure de damunt,
de què us val, doncs, poetes, la poesia?

EL POETA

Alguna veu jo sento en aquest punt
580 que d'altre modo no la sentiria.

ADALAISA

Oh! La veu sense so del que és difunt!
No és pas aquesta la que jo voldria:
aquella eixida de mon pit de carn
que alegrement entorn me ressonava:
585 aquella, amic, és la que jo et deman,
i lo demés que amb ella es comportava.
I si ta poesia no pot tant,
si no em pots tornar al món, calla i acaba.

EL POETA

Adalaisa, Adalaisa, per pietat,
590 al temps hi ha encara coses no sabudes;
la poesia tot just ha començat
i és plena de virtuts inconegudes.
Mes ara tens raó, prou hem parlat,
esperem en silenci altres vingudes.

You take me for defunct, I take me for alive;
And just as if I had been buried quite alive,
575 The wanting in my senses rages on,
Yet there is something here that thwarts it.
If you can't free me from its tyranny,
What good to you, then, poets, is your poetry?

POET

I hear a voice on its occasion
580 I wouldn't hear in any other way.

ADALAISA

Ah! The voice of those now dead, soundless!
That's not the voice for me:
The voice that outed from my chest of flesh
And echoed joyfully around me—
585 That's the voice I ask you for, my friend:
And all that came with it.
And if your poetry can't cut it,
If you can't return me to the world, muzzle it.

POET

Please, please, Adalaisa,
590 There are things that elude us in our time;
Poetry has just begun:
It holds out virtues still unknown.
But you're right, we've talked enough,
Let's wait, quietly, for what comes up.

FROM SEQUENCES
(*SEQÜÈNCIES*, 1911)

Maragall's fifth and final book of poems would not appear until five years after *Enllà* (1906). During this period, from 1906 to 1911, although one of intense literary activity for Maragall, he off-centers himself from the limelight, devoting his energy to translating: Novalis's *Heinrich von Ofterdingen* (*Enric d'Ofterdingen*, 1907), Pindar's *Olympian I* (*Olímpica I*, 1910) and Goethe's *Maxims and Reflections* (*Pensaments de Goethe*, 1910); to reflecting on poetry: *Elogi de la poesia* (1909); to completing his tragedy in verse *Nausica* (1910, based on the character Nausicaa from Homer's *Odyssey*) and beginning his verse translation of *Homeric Hymns* (1910-11); and to collaborating sporadically with the press (having left in 1906 *Diario de Barcelona* for the second time) (Casals 1998, 715). It is not until the wake of the Setmana Tràgica (Tragic Week) of 26-30 July 1909 that Maragall's reaction to the shattering events of that week and its grim consequences would catapult him into the public spotlight like never before. Maragall's three seminal essays on the Setmana Tràgica—"Ah! Barcelona," "City of Pardon," and "The Church After Burning" (all three included in this selection)—serve as indispensable auxiliary texts for sounding the depths of his extraordinary poem "New Ode to Barcelona," a re-foundational palimpsest bearing in part the stamp of towering Catalan Renaixença poet Jacint Verdaguer's (1845-1902) no less extraordinary 1883 poem "A Barcelona" ("To Barcelona," see Puppo 2007, 174-189, 318-322; see also, Puppo 2016), yet departing from it radically to challenge the entrenched state of moral complacency in the face of the social meltdown concomitant to the Setmana Tràgica and its wake (see below, this headnote, and endnotes to "New Ode to Barcelona" and the three articles mentioned above).

As for the title, *Seqüències* (Sequences), Maragall pointed out in a letter to writer and historian Carles Rahola (1881-1939) how "nearly all [the poems] are follow-ups on previous inspirations, especially a third and I'd say concluding part to *El comte Arnau*" (Maragall 1911a, 1082; quoted in Casals 1998, 721, and Abrams 2010, 382). Furthermore, both Casals and Abrams concur in the intriguing observation that the title also echoes the cinematographic quality of the volume's poetic imagery; Casals remarks on the cover design, featuring "small squares which, unless my imagination distorts my reading, might represent the perforations along the edges of film" (720); Abrams, likewise, enumerates several pre-film animation devices with which Maragall was surely acquainted (the magic lantern, zoetrope, flip book, Kinetoscope), culminating in the early motion picture cameras of the 1890s—the Lumière brothers, Abrams notes, demonstrated their cinematograph in Barcelona in 1896 (384).

The brevity of the volume is addressed by Maragall in a letter to friend Lluís Lluís:

Truly, for being all my poetic work of five years, it is small, but those moments of poetry that I feel intensely are few; and I do not wish to set down in verse any others; and all the more when my book is for the public that I reject those I find insufficiently alive. (Maragall 1911b, 914; quoted in Casals 1998, 721)

Nor, in fact, were quite all the poems in the volume penned precisely during the period 1906-1911; "La sirena" ("The Siren") to mention one, appeared in the magazine *Juventut* in January 1905; conversely, a number of poems whose composition corresponds to the period were not included (see Casals 1998, 721).

The carefully screened poems in the volume are organized into four sections along a continuum, observes Casals, of "progressive degrees of 'transcendence' both personal and collective" (722). In the first section, titled *Seguit de les vistes al mar* (Continuing Views of the Sea; not included in this selection), the series poem of the same title takes up again the seascape motif of "Vistes al mar" (*Enllà*) and numerous other earlier poems. Curiously, this first section's only other poem following, "La fageda d'en Jordà" ("The Beech Woods of Jordà"), seems to clash with the seascape motif. The apparent in-congruousness of a woodscape among seascapes has drawn various critical responses. Casals (722) notes that Maragall sojourns in Olot (near the location of the woods) in midsummer, amounting to a side trip from the seashore holiday at Caldes d'Estrach, to which he returns for the remainder of the summer holiday; thus seen, remarks Casals, the "beech woods are the prolongation of, and prelude to the sea," evoking continuity in lieu of interruption, and depicted as "green as waters deep and clear" (poem, line 5). For his part, Abrams (400) points out how "La fageda d'en Jordà" breaks not with the seascape motif, but rather with the mold of Maragall's other poe-tic reflections on his mountain excursions, generally characterized by significantly conflictive elements; in contrast, the beech woods give rise to the "harmony, serenity and equilibrium" of Maragall's seascapes. Additionally, the exceptional quality of "La fageda d'en Jordà" with respect to other Maragall poems of mountain or inland excursions is mirrored in the exceptional geographical phenomenon that are the woods themselves, which, remarks Abrams, grow—surprisingly—at an altitude much lower than their customary habitat.

The second section, titled *Represa d'Haidé i altres* (Retake of Haidé and Other Poems), comprises six rather short poems, the first and longest of which is "Represa d'Haidé" (not included in this selection), a follow-up on "Haidé," written some ten years earlier (published in *Les disperses*, 1904); laborious research by Casals (2011a) to uncover the identity of the mysterious woman referred to by Maragall as "Haidé" seems to have proven fruitful, pointing in all probability to Marie Marguerite Laborde (1880-1973), French writer who sometimes used the pen names "Andrée Béarn" and "Hein?" and whom Maragall must have met during summer sojourns in Cauterets from 1901 to 1906; Laborde married well-known Catalan artist and poet Alexandre de Riquer (1856-1920) in September 1911 (52-53).

It is this second section's third poem, "La sirena" ("The Siren"), that we include in this selection. Dating the poem's composition between 1902 and 1904, Casals links the appearance on the bleak cityscape of workers absent from their factories with, on the one hand, the lockouts of 1900-1901, or alternatively, the general strike of February 1902 (1998, 764-765); both work stoppages would have provided Maragall with the raw material for his hard-hitting imagery of the factory workers, adrift and alienated, depicted in the poem. Particularly disconcerting—and effective—is Maragall's evocation, where the displaced workers are concerned, of the disconnectedness of the human spirit both outside and inside the home. With the stark pathos of its social gaze, "The Siren" echoes "Fatherhood" (*Poesies*) and prefigures the extraordinary "New Ode to Barcelona" (below).

With the Setmana Tràgica (Tragic Week) of July 1909, the spiritual and social crises of late nineteenth-century Barcelona would give way to a full-blown social meltdown. The three articles (included in the prose section of this selection) written by Maragall for Barcelona newspapers amounted to a bold call to his fellow citizens to first: examine their consciences as to the underlying causes of the turmoil which had left over a hundred dead (see Benet 2009, 61); second, call for a stop to the military tribunals and subsequent summary executions of civilians—Maragall's fellow citizens were quick to pin the blame for the deaths and destruction on scapegoats: the city's underclass and their unwelcome champions, including renowned educator Francesc Ferrer i Guàrdia (1854-1909), who, having taken no part in the revolt, was sentenced to death by a military tribunal in view of his anarchist leanings and executed on 13 October 1909 (the international campaign on Ferrer i Guàrdia's behalf led to the fall, that same month, of Spain's prime minister Antonio Maura); and third, Maragall challenged his fellow citizens to reexamine the meaning of the Christian faith that they purported to practice. The poem "Oda nova a Barcelona" ("New Ode to Barcelona") encapsulates the critical energy of the three articles, powerfully poeticizing Maragall's throwing down of the gauntlet in the face of the citizenry's complacency. The genesis of the first section of the poem (lines one through twenty-five, dated 4 February 1909) stems from the celebrated prize-winning project proposed by Occitan architect and urban planner Léon Jaussely (1875-1933) to modernize the city (see Casals 1998, 779-782). The remainder of the poem (lines twenty-six through one hundred) would be written in the wake of the Setmana Tràgica; shunning, now, all pretense of conventional prosodic formality (the pre-Setmana Tràgica stanzas feature Catalan alexandrines of Verdaguerian stamp), Maragall shapeshifts his decrial, at the poem's turning point, to accommodate the form to its new disruptive tenor and remonstrative content. Strikingly, and coupled with the break in formal prosodic convention, Maragall—in contrast to his predecessor Verdaguer's "To Barcelona" (1883), in which the explicit enumeration of important places and events pointed to the outward manifestation of a collective inner life—avoids, in his re-foundational update, "New Ode to Barcelona," explicit denotation of places and events, signaling the need for an inward turn and crucial examination of that same collective inner life (see Puppo 2016). Finally, the importance of "Oda nova a Barcelona" at this crucial moment in the city's history is floodlighted in the volume by Maragall's emplacement of it as the single poem in the third section, identically titled *Oda nova a Barcelona*.

The concluding section of *Seqüències* features two poems: "La fi del comte l'Arnau" ("The End of Count Arnau") and "Cant espiritual" ("Spiritual"). Between 1907 and 1910, Maragall brought his Count Arnau cycle to completion. Quintana notes:

Moreover, the case of Maragall and Count Arnau was a rather peculiar one. Indeed, Count Arnau became a weighty character, one that was difficult to shake off, similar to the way Faust pursued Goethe throughout his life. Thus, the character underwent changes along with the poet, and we see reflected in the various parts of the poem the main concerns of Maragall at the respective times of publication. (1997, 12)

In "The End of Count Arnau" the question of redemption is raised and poetically resolved not only as it relates to Arnau (and "humanity" at large into the mix), but also for the Poet, who, we may recall, stood at a loss for words at the end of part two. But it will be through song—a "living voice" (popular, traditional song sprung from the land and ordinary people)—that redemption will finally come. It is important to note, however, that the song has changed. No longer is it the one transcribed in one hundred ninety-two lines (not included in this selection) by Maragall and inserted in part two as section II, "La cançó del comte l'Arnau." It is now a "strange new song" sung by a shepherdess who "has completely changed the tune." The popular song that had given rise to the legend (not the reverse; see Romeu 2000, 5-15; Quintana 1997, 10-11) and, in turn, poetry, has been transformed and come full circle in a symbolic cycle whose components—popular song, legend, poetry—nourish each other; and significantly, the Poet of part two is re-empowered within the cycle.

Maragall's late-life landmark poem "Cant espiritual" ("Spiritual") caught the eye of Albert Camus (1913-1960) and Eugenio Montale (1896-1981), whose French and Italian translations of this powerful and lovingly agnostic poem appeared, respectively, in 1957 and 1975. Maragall's poem looms large in a long-standing tradition of Catalan-language works invoking or interpellating the divinity and transcendence, from renowned Mallorcan medieval philosopher, theologian and writer Ramon Llull (c. 1232-1316) and Valencian poet Ausiàs March (1400-1459) to any number of nineteenth- to twenty-first century poets; other precedents with which Maragall was familiar include the "Song of Songs" of the Old Testament, "Cántico espiritual" by St. John of the Cross (1542-1591) and works by Maragall's beloved Goethe (1749-1832) and Novalis (1772-1801), as well as his esteemed friend Miguel de Unamuno (1864-1936) (see Abrams 2010, 448-449; Casals 1998, 813). Throughout "Spiritual" readers will catch echoes from numerous other Maragall poems that call into question the tenets of dogmatic transcendence, favoring and celebrating instead the joy and conviviality of living in the world.

LA FAGEDA D'EN JORDÀ

Saps on és la fageda d'en Jordà?
Si vas pels volts d'Olot, amunt del pla,
trobaràs un indret verd i profond
com mai cap més n'hagis trobat al món;
5   un verd com d'aigua endins, profond i clar;
el verd de la fageda d'en Jordà.

El caminant, quan entra en aquest lloc,
comença a caminar-hi a poc a poc;
compta els seus passos en la gran quietud:
10   s'atura, i no sent res, i està perdut.

Li agafa un dolç oblit de tot lo món
en el silenci d'aquell lloc profond,
i no pensa en sortir, o hi pensa en va:
és pres de la fageda d'en Jordà,
15   presoner del silenci i la verdor.

Oh companyia! Oh deslliurant presó!

THE BEECH WOODS OF JORDÀ

You know the beech woods called Jordà?
Out by Olot, above the plain,
you'll come to a spot that's deep and green;
it's not like any you've ever seen:
5   it's green as waters deep and clear,
the green of the beech woods of Jordà.
The walker, entering these woods,
proceeds at a pace that's easy and slow,
counting the steps in the quiet stillness:
10   and stopping, hears nothing, and now is lost.
A sweet oblivion of the world takes hold
in the silence that governs that deep spot,
no thought of escape—pointless anyway:
held among the beeches of Jordà
15   captive to silence and green.
This fellowship! This liberating prison!

LA SIRENA (FRAGMENT)

....

Comença al cel l'eterna provatura
de la llum renaixent…

       Per terra, fosca enllà,
el xiscle ardent de la sirena impura
5   crida an els pobres cap a treballar.

No ets pas ben bé com la sirena antiga,
altrament cantadora; mes, semblant,
quan amb ta veu d'imperiosa amiga
fas acudir la gent al teu voltant.
10   I, si volen fugir del teu imperi,
roden per la ciutat esmaperduts:
van pels barris dels rics sense saber-hi,
arrossegant els peus, tots desvalguts.
Les bruses la ciutat enterboleixen,
15   s'estenen per les vies dels palaus:
als fills de llurs suades no coneixen
i se'ls contemplen amb tristor d'esclaus.
I tu, a l'altre matí, tornes irada
el teu xiscle a llançar imperiós;
20   mes no et reïx: la turba esgarriada
s'entossudeix en un silenci ombrós.
I calles tu a la fi; ja més no els crides:
s'aixequen albes en una gran quietud,
i en les cases dels pobres, entristides,
25   hi ha una mena de pau sense virtut.

THE SIREN (FRAGMENT)

....

In the sky there begins the timeless trial
of light reborn…

          Out over the land, from the darkness,
the scorching whistle of the tainted siren
5   calls the poor to work.

You're not quite like the sirens of old,
whose song was another; and yet, similar,
when in that voice of unignorable friend
you summon all around you.
10 And should they wish to flee your dominions,
they roam the city aimlessly:
they wander, adrift, the precincts of the rich,
dragging their feet, destitute.
Their factory smocks bespatter the city,
15 outspreading through streets lined with mansions:
they do not know the children of their toil,
and gaze on them with the gloom of the enslaved.
And you, next morning, in a fit of anger
let go again your ruthless whistle;
20 but it's no use: the straying throngs
sink stubbornly into a dismal silence.
And finally, you're silent too; you call them no longer:
the dawns break in stark stillness,
and in the homes of the poor, thick with gloom,
25 there reigns a peace that has no virtue.

En hores desusades assegut
el nin mira estranyat el pare a casa,
com si s'hagués tornat festa tot dia,
com si tot l'any fos un seguit estrany
30 de diumenges en sense l'alegria.

....

A boy, puzzled, sees his father
sitting at home an unaccustomed hour,
as if every day were now a holiday,
as if the whole year were a strange succession
30   of Sundays empty of any joy.

....

ODA NOVA A BARCELONA

—On te'n vas, Barcelona, esperit català
que has vençut la carena i has saltat ja la tanca
i te'n vas dret enfora amb tes cases disperses,
lo mateix que embriagada de tan gran llibertat?

5   —Veig allà el Pirineu amb ses neus somrosades,
i al davant Catalunya tota estesa als seus peus,
i me'n vaig… És l'amor qui m'empeny cap enfora,
i me'n vaig delirant amb els braços oberts.

—Oh! detura't un punt! Mira el mar, Barcelona,
10   com te faixa de blau fins al baix horitzó,
els poblets blanquejant tot al llarg de la costa,
que se'n van plens de sol vorejant la blavor.
I tu fuges del mar?…
               —Vinc del mar i l'estimo,
i he pujat aquí dalt per mirar-lo millor,
15   i me'n vaig i no em moc: sols estenc els meus braços
perquè vull Catalunya tota a dintre el meu cor.

—Altra mar veus enllà, encrespada i immòbil,
de les serres que riuen al sol dolçament:
per copsar tanta terra i tanta mar, Barcelona,
20   ja et caldrà un pit ben gran, amb uns braços ben ferms.

—Com més terra i més mar i més pobles obiro,
a mesura d'amor el meu pit s'engrandeix,
i me sento una força que abans no tenia,
i sóc tan tota una altra que fins jo em desconec.

NEW ODE TO BARCELONA

"Where to now, Barcelona, Catalan spirit,
That you've conquered your mountains and leapt your walls
As outward you venture, your houses far-spreading,
As though by your own great freedom enthralled?"

5   "The far-off Pyrenees blush with snow,
And facing, Catalonia stretched at her feet,
And so, driven by love, outward I go,
Onward with arms spread wide, half-frenzied."

"But wait! Think of your sea, Barcelona,
10   Sashing you in blue to the low horizon,
And your villages glimmering along the coast,
Edging the azure and washed in the sun.
And you'd turn from the sea?"
                      "From my cherished sea I come,
And the better to watch her I've climbed up this far;
15   I set out, yet remain: merely opening my arms
For all Catalonia to hold in my heart."

"In the distance, that other sea swells in stillness,
Its ranging peaks sparkling soft in the sun:
To contain such a land and its sea, Barcelona,
20   Your breast must be generous, your arms robust."

"The more land and more sea and more towns I take in,
To the measure of love, my breast grows the greater,
And I feel such strength never felt before this,
And I'm so much another, I seem like a stranger."

25 —Corre enllà, corre enllà, corre enllà, Barcelona,
que ja et cal esser una altra per esser la que deus;
perquè ets alta i airosa i fas molta planta,
però bé et falta encara molt més del que tens.

Ets covarda i crudel i grollera,
30 Barcelona, però ets riallera
perquè tens un bell cel al damunt;
vanitosa, arrauxada i traçuda;
ets una menestrala pervinguda
que ho fa tot per punt.

35 Alces molts gallarets i penons i oriflames,
molts llorers, moltes palmes,
banderes a l'aire i domassos al sol,
i remous a grans crits tes espesses gentades
per qualsevulga cosa acorruades
40 entorn de qualsevol.

Mes, passada l'estona i el dia i la rauxa
i el vent de disbauxa, de tot te desdius;
i abandones la via i la glòria i l'empresa,
i despulles el gran de grandesa.
45 I encara te'n rius.

Te presums i engavanyes alhora
amb manto de monja i vestit de senyora
i vel de la musa i floc relluent;
pro mudes de pressa, i amb gran gosadia
50 la musa i la nimfa i la dama i la pia
s'arrenca el postís i la veu disfressada,
i surt la marmanyera endiablada

25   "Stretch far, stretch far, stretch far, Barcelona,
for you must be another to be what you ought;
how true you are tall and graceful and handsome,
but you're lacking in more, so much more than you've got.

"You're a coward, you're cruel and you're vulgar,
30   Barcelona, but you're cheerful,
since above you there shines a bright sky;
boastful, impetuous and shrewd:
you're a guildswoman arrivée
bullheaded in everything you do.

35   "You raise lots of banners and pennants and streamers,
and loads of laurels and palms,
flags hoisted high and damasks in the sun,
and you stir up your shouting, pressing crowds,
all gathering for no telling what,
40   all keen on there's no telling who.

"But after the heat of the hour and the day
and the winds of unreason subside, you recoil;
and you fly from boulevard and glory and deed,
and you strip the great of their greatness.
45   And for encore, you laugh it off.

"You presume and yet rein yourself in all at once,
fit out in nun's shawl and lady's gown,
a muse's veil and showy ribbons;
but your moods change quickly, and boldly
50   the muse and the nymph and the lady and the nun
shed the getup and counterfeit voice,
and out comes the devil's handmaid

que empaita la monja i li crema el convent…
I després el refàs més potent!

55   Esclata la mort de tes vies rialleres
en l'aire suau:
esclata impensada, i segura i traïdora
com altra riallada escarnidora…
Riallades de sang!
60   El fang dels teus carrers, oh Barcelona!
és pastat amb sang.
I tens dreta en la mar la muntanya, ai! que venja
amb son castell al cim, i amb la revenja
mes ai! en el flanc!

65   Tens aquesta Rambla que és una hermosura…
i tens la dolçura dels teus arravals,
on, tan prop de tes vies sonores
i al mig de les boires del fum i ses marques,
camps de blat en la pau dels patriarques
70   maduren lentament els fruits anyals.
I allí, a quatre passes, febrosa de sobres,
més ampla que l'altra, la Rambla dels pobres
tremola en la fosca ses llums infernals.

Pro ni el baf ni la pols de tos llots i desferres,
75   ni els pals i filferres
que t'armen a sobre la gran teranyina,
ni el fumar de tes mil xemeneies,
ni el flam de les teies
que mou la discòrdia i abranden l'incendi,
80   són bastants a posar vilipendi

to hunt down the nun and set fire to the convent…
and then you rebuild it, redoubled in strength!

55 "Death strikes in the mild breeze
of your cheerful streets:
it comes unexpected, certain, treacherous
like another boisterous outburst of laughter…
Boisterous blood!
60 The mud of your streets, Barcelona,
has blood in its mix.
And straight from the sea stands your mountain, wreaking
vengeance high in its castle, and revenge
aimed at the ribs!

65 "You have your Rambla, a thing of beauty,
and your placid outlying districts,
where, not far from your humming streets
and amid the sifting smoke of your enterprise,
wheatfields bask in the peace of patriarchs,
70 ripening slowly the year's harvest.
And there, steps away, fevering for scraps
and broader than the other, the poorer Rambla
flickers her infernal lamps in the darkness.

"Not the stench or the dust of your sludge and your rubble,
75 not power lines on poles
floating above you a thick-tangling web,
not the smoke from your thousand chimneys,
not the fires of your torches
bunching in strife and setting off flames,
80 are enough to revile

an aquest cel que tens tan dolç i blau
que tot s'ho empassa i resol i canvia,
i ho torna en oblit i consol i alegria:
mil cops la perdesses,
85 mil cops més tornaria a tu la pau.

A la part de Llevant, místic exemple,
com una flor gegant floreix un temple
meravellat d'haver nascut aquí,
entremig d'una gent tan sorruda i dolenta,
90 que se'n riu i flastoma i es baralla i s'esventa
contra tot lo humà i lo diví.
Mes, enmig la misèria i la ràbia i fumera,
el temple (tant se val!) s'alça i prospera
esperant uns fidels que han de venir.

95 Tal com ets, tal te vull, ciutat mala:
és com un mal donat, de tu s'exhala,
que ets vana i coquina i traïdora i grollera,
que ens fa abaixar el rostre
Barcelona!, i amb tos pecats, nostra! nostra!
100 Barcelona nostra! la gran encisera!

your skies, so soft and so blue,
ingesting all things, smoothing and shifting,
and bringing oblivion, solace and joy:
and were it lost a thousand times,
85   a thousand times would peace revisit you.

"In your eastern quarters, mystic's wonder,
there blooms gigantic, flowerlike—a temple:
marveling at having been born right here,
among such wicked and peevish people,
90   who mock and curse and quarrel and rail
against everything human and divine.
Still, amid the misery and the wrath and the fumes,
the temple rises, all the same, and thrives,
awaiting the faithful to come.

95   "I'll take you as you are, wretched city:
it's as though you cast an evil gaze—
you're vain, mean, traitorous and coarse,
and you fill us with shame,
Barcelona, and yet with your sins you're all ours:
100   ours, Barcelona, Grand Enchantress!"

FROM EL COMTE ARNAU
(TERCERA PART: LA FI DEL COMTE L'ARNAU)

Totes les veus de la terra
se fan sentir an el comte Arnau,
li van movent eterna guerra
100 per els camins de la gran pau.
Són com a mar esvalotada
que de molt lluny se fa present
amb la clamor de ses onades
tota la nit en gran turment;
105 són com el vent de les altures
que d'un sol crit omple l'espai;
són com el plor de les criatures,
que no té fi ni en tindrà mai;
són el Dolor, rei de la terra,
110 que en tot pit d'home es fa sentir...
El comte Arnau se desespera
perquè vol dir-lo i no el sap dir.

Però l'esposa fila i canta,
dalt a mig aire del cel blau.
115 El comte Arnau tot s'hi decanta
per si la sent cantar suau.
Mes a sa veu altra es conlliga
que mai s'hi havia conlligat...
que va cantant la cançó antiga
120 amb una nova pietat.
És una veu encara viva.

FROM COUNT ARNAU

(PART THREE: THE END OF COUNT ARNAU)

All the voices of the earth
Now resound for Count Arnau,
They wage eternal war on him
100 Along the paths of lasting sleep:
They are like on some troubled sea
Whose far-off din of waves has now
Come clamoring in close by
In agony throughout the night;
105 Or like the winds that blow up high
And fill the skies in a single cry;
Or like the crying of babies
That never ends, and never will;
They are Sorrow, king of the earth,
110 And felt inside all breasts of men…
Count Arnau is losing heart:
He would, but cannot, put it in words.

Meanwhile, his wife spins and sings
High midway in the blue sky.
115 Count Arnau bends himself upward,
And strains to catch her gentle song.
But now a new voice blends with hers,
One that he's never heard before—
A voice that sings the ancient song:
120 Sings it with a new devotion.
It's a voice that is still living.

No ve del cel, ni ve dels llimbs:
ve de la terra, tan festiva,
amb verd als camps i amb sol als cims.

125 En un pendís de la muntanya
hi ha una pastora de l'ull blau
que, tot cantant la cançó estranya,
se'l va estimant, el comte Arnau.

Un campanar sona en l'altura;
130 les gents se mouen pels sembrats;
esquellejant salta i pastura
l'escampadissa dels ramats…

I la pastora enamorada
canta que canta la cançó:
135 li ha mudat tota la tonada
i ha redimit el pecador.

Que, des de que ella l'ha cantada
amb altra veu, amb altre acord,
jo no hi ha *ànima damnada…*

140 La cançó ha mort, la cançó ha mort.

Seguiu el pla, seguiu la serra,
vila i poblat, per on vulgueu:
la cançó és fora de la terra
i ja mai més la sentireu.

145 Alguns diran que la sentiren;
altres ni en tenen cap record;
quins l'oblidaren, quins ni l'oïren…

La cançó ha mort, la cançó ha mort.

Jo, d'una vella ja afollada
150 pel pes dels anys, la vaig sentir
ja sense to, a glops, trencada…

It doesn't come from heaven, or limbo:
But from the bright and festive earth
With fields of green and sunlit summits.
125 There, on an easy mountain slope,
There walks a blue-eyed shepherdess,
Who while she sings the strange new song,
She brings Arnau into her heart.
A bell tower rings out from the heights;
130 People stir on ripening fields;
Scatterings of flocks with clunky bells
Graze and frolick over pastures…
And love stirs in the shepherdess
As on and on she sings the song:
135 She has completely changed the tune
And she's redeemed the one who sinned.
Ever since she sings the song—
Gives it new voice and harmony,
No longer is the *soul condemned*…
140 The song has died, the song is dead.
Over the plains or high in the mountains,
In cities and towns, be where you might:
The song is now gone from the earth
And never to be heard again.
145 Now some might say that they have heard it,
And others that they can't recall it;
Some have forgotten, some never noticed…
The song has died, the song is dead.
I once heard an old woman sing it,
150 Fuddled by the weight of her years,
But it was tuneless, fitful, patchy…

I aquella vella es va morir.

Cantant, cantant, nasqué la infàmia,
i descantant, la redempció:
155 el comte Arnau tenia l'ànima
a la mercè d'una cançó.

Lo que la mort tanca i captiva,
sols per la vida és deslliurat:
basta una noia amb la veu viva
160 per redimir la humanitat.

And the woman has long since died.
By dint of the song there came disgrace,
And by its unsinging, redemption:
155 The soul of Count Arnau was held
At the mercy of a song.
What death takes into custody
Only life can set free:
One living voice is all it takes
160 To redeem humanity.

CANT ESPIRITUAL

Si el món ja és tan formós, Senyor, si es mira
amb la pau vostra a dintre de l'ull nostre,
què més ens podeu dar en una altra vida?

Perxò estic tan gelós dels ulls, i el rostre,
i el cos que m'heu donat, Senyor, i el cor
que s'hi mou sempre… i temo tant la mort!

¿Amb quins altres sentits me'l fareu veure
aquest cel blau damunt de les muntanyes,
i el mar immens, i el sol que pertot brilla?
Deu-me en aquests sentits l'eterna pau
i no voldré més cel que aquest cel blau.

Aquell que a cap moment li digué «—Atura't»
sinó al mateix que li dugué la mort,
jo no l'entenc, Senyor; jo, que voldria
aturar a tants moments de cada dia
per fé'ls eterns a dintre del meu cor!…
O és que aquest «fer etern» és ja la mort?
Mes llavores, la vida, què seria?
¿Fóra només l'ombra del temps que passa,
i la il·lusió del lluny i de l'aprop,
el compte de lo molt, i el poc, i el massa,
enganyador, perquè ja tot ho és tot?

Tant se val! Aquest món, sia com sia,
tan divers, tan extens, tan temporal;
aquesta terra, amb tot lo que s'hi cria,

SPIRITUAL

If the world is so fine, Lord, if we see it
with the peace that is yours in our eyes,
what more could you give us in another life?

That's why I cling to these eyes, this face,
5   this body you've given me, Lord, and this heart
stirring nonstop inside—I'm so afraid of death!

With what other senses would you have me see
the blue sky over the mountains,
and the vast sea, and sun shining down on it all?
10 In these my senses give me peace everlasting
and I'll want no more heaven than blue skies.

Those who never said to any moment: "Stop!"
except for the one that brought them death,
I can't understand, Lord; I who would gladly
15 stop so many moments every day
and have them go on forever in my heart!
Or is this "go on forever" to be death?
But what, then, would life be?
Would it be but the shadow of time's passing,
20 the illusion of things far-off and near,
a tallying up the many, the few, the too much—
delusory, because everything's all there is?

No matter! This world, be what it might,
so varied, so wide, so bound in time;
25 this earth, with all that thrives here,

és ma pàtria, Senyor: i ¿no podria
esser també una pàtria celestial?
Home só i és humana ma mesura
per tot quant puga creure i esperar:
30   si ma fe i ma esperança aquí s'atura,
me'n fareu una culpa més enllà?
Més enllà veig el cel i les estrelles,
i encara allí voldria esser-hi hom:
si heu fet les coses a mos ulls tan belles,
35   si heu fet mos ulls i mos sentits per elles,
per què aclucà'ls cercant un altre *com*?
Si per mi com aquest no n'hi haurà cap!
Ja ho sé que sou, Senyor; pro on sou, qui ho sap?
Tot lo que veig se vos assembla en mi...
40   Deixeu-me creure, doncs, que sou aquí.
I quan vinga aquella hora de temença
en què s'acluquin aquests ulls humans,
obriu-me'n, Senyor, uns altres de més grans
per contemplar la vostra faç immensa.
45   Sia'm la mort una major naixença!

is my home, Lord; and mightn't
it be, as well, a heavenly home?
I am a man and my measure is human
in all I might come to believe and hope:
30 and if my faith and hope end here,
will you fault me in the beyond?
I see, out there, the sky and stars—
and there, too, one wishes to be:
if you've made things so delightful to my eyes,
35 and fit me out for them with sight and senses,
why strip me of them for some other how of it?
Like this one, for me, there'll never be another!
I know that you are, Lord; but where? who can say?
All that I see resembles you in me…
40 Let me believe, then, that you're here.
And when the dreaded hour comes
and these my human eyes are shut,
open in me, Lord, new and greater ones
so I might see your face in its immensity.
45 Let my death be a farther-reaching birth!

PROSE

Our selection of Maragall's extensive prose works is limited in this volume, yet we are convinced that the texts chosen here are representative of Maragall's stature as a prominent *intellectuel engagé* of his times; in this case, both in challenging his readers to reflect on the social turmoil and repression during and after the Setmana Tràgica (Tragic Week) of 26-31 July 1909, and in his correspondence with renowned thinkers Miguel de Unamuno (1864-1936) and José Ortega y Gasset (1883-1955).

The Setmana Tràgica articles

In synthesis, the three articles written for Barcelona newspapers in the wake of the Setmana Tràgica amounted to a bold call by Maragall to his readers to take three actions: in the first, "Ah! Barcelona…" (1 October 1909) to examine their consciences as to the underlying causes of the turmoil which left more than a hundred dead (Benet [1963] 2009, 61); second, to call for a stop to the military tribunals and summary executions of civilians—Maragall's fellow citizens were quick to pin the blame for the deaths and destruction on scapegoats: the city's underclass and their unwelcome champions. These included the renowned educator Francesc Ferrer i Guàrdia (1854-1909), who, having taken no part in the revolt, was sentenced to death by a military tribunal in view of his anarchist leanings and executed on 13 October 1909 (the international campaign on behalf of Ferrer i Guàrdia led to the fall, that same month, of Spain's prime minister Antonio Maura). In his proposed third action, Maragall challenged citizens to re-examine the meaning of the Christian faith that they purported to practice.

Maragall's second article on the Setmana Tràgica, "La ciutat del perdó" ("City of Pardon"), would not be published. Submitted on 10 October—three days before the execution of Ferrer i Guàrdia—it was quietly ignored by the editor-in-chief of *La Veu de Catalunya*, Enric Prat de la Riba (1870-1917). In it Maragall appealed for clemency on behalf of Ferrer i Guàrdia and others facing the death sentence. Maragall, reminding his would-be readers that Barcelona was at that time widely known as the "city of bombs," urged them to call for clemency so that Barcelona might now be known as the "city of pardon," and adding that "from that moment on [Barcelona] would begin to be a city."

The third article, "L'església cremada" ("The Church After Burning") was published in *La Veu de Catalunya* on 18 December 1909. Some two weeks after its publication, Maragall commented on reactions to the article in a letter to his friend Miguel de Unamuno (dated 31 December, included in this selection). The article was met with public silence:

[N]o one dared to attack Maragall publicly, as he was at that time Catalonia's most prestigious and most respected writer, and no one could cast doubt on his Catholicism. No Catholic publication, nor publication on the right, reproduced, commented on, or mentioned the article at that time. It was long met with total silence. (Benet 199)

Even Bishop Josep Torras i Bages (1846-1916), in his annual Christmas greeting to Maragall, refrained from making mention of the article (Benet 200). There did appear, however, a long anonymous article published on the front page of *El Progreso* (20 December 1909) which attacked Maragall under the title "Palabras de un Cristiano: Apología de la Revolución." Writer Cosme Vidal (aka Josep Aladern, 1869-1918) countered the anonymous article with a defense of Maragall published four days later in the same newspaper (see Benet 202-205). (For further details in English on Maragall's Setmana Tràgica writings, see Puppo 2012a; 2016.)

Maragall's letters to Unamuno. Reply to Ortega y Gasset
The collection of letters kept at the Joan Maragall Archive numbers over one thousand documents sent and received, including twenty-five letters from Unamuno and twenty sent by Maragall to Unamuno from 1900 to 1911, two of which we include here: Maragall's second letter to Unamuno and his seventeenth, dated 6 November 1902, and 31 December 1909, respectively.

In the first letter we present here (6 November 1902) Maragall makes reference to what is known as Unamuno's Cartagena Speech. Maragall goes on to praise Unamuno's second novel, *Amor y pedagogía* (1902; Love and Teaching), before responding to Unamuno's query regarding charges brought by a military tribunal against Maragall for his article "La patria nueva" (11 September 1902; The New Country). In his previous letter (3 November) Unamuno, who had recently read the article, expressed his bewilderment: "No acierto a comprender como pudieron encarcelarle por escrito tan llano, tan sincero, tan noble y tan patriótico, en cualquier sentido racional en que esta palabra se tome." ("I fail to see how they could put you in jail for writing an article so straightforward, so sincere, so noble, and so patriotic in any rational sense of the word.") The subsequent reference to "Domènech" and "Robert" comes in the context of the political scene prior to the legislative and municipal elections held earlier that year; the politically active architect Lluís Domènech i Montaner (1849-1923) and physician Bartomeu Robert i Yarzábal (aka Doctor Robert, 1842-1902) were among the public figures known as the "four presidents" (all were former presidents of civic and business associations) who backed the conservative pro-Catalan Lliga Regionalista in the elections. In his previous letter Unamuno had also mentioned he was working on a new novel, *La tía*, published many years later as *La tía Tula* (1921) (*Aunt Tula*, translated by Stanley Appelbaum, 2005).

Maragall's letter of 31 December 1909 (in reply to Unamuno's letter dated 28 December) makes reference to "the mad lover" and "the dead queen," characters in Unamuno's comedy *La princesa doña Lambra* (1909), which Unamuno mentions was playing at the Teatro Lara; "Ors" refers to writer and critic Eugeni d'Ors (1881-1954), a prominent figure of Noucentisme, the literary and artistic movement that succeeded and opposed Modernisme. Prior to his letter of 28 December, Unamuno had not written Maragall since April of the previous year, and now informs him that he was in Bilbao during the events of the Tragic Week: "yo vivo con el espiritu más en Bilbao que en esta Salamanca. En Bilbao estaba durante la semana trágica." ("I live with my spirit in Bilbao more than here in Salamanca. I was in Bilbao during the tragic week.") Maragall remarks on the reactions to his recent article "The Church After Burning" published in *La Veu de Catalunya* on 18 December. Maragall then encourages Unamuno to make the quiet visit to Barcelona that he spoke of in his last letter:

"Cuánto deseo volver ahí! Pero silenciosa y furtivamente, sin empresa ni anuncio, no a hablar sino a oír, a ver, a vivir." ("How I wish to return! But quietly and secretly, unencumbered and unannounced, not to speak but only to listen, to see, to live.") La Solidaritat, or La Solidaritat Catalana, was a broad coalition of pro-Catalan parties under the leadership of Enric Prat de la Riba (1870-1917) that won a sweeping victory in the 1907 general elections.

The article "La verdadera cuestión previa" ("The Real Preliminary Question") was written by way of reply to José Ortega y Gasset's article "Diputado por la cultura," published in the Madrid daily *El Imparcial* (28 May 1910), and reproduced in the magazine *La Cataluña* (11 June 1910), where it came to Maragall's attention (see Sotelo Vázquez 2016). Instead of publishing it, however, Maragall enclosed it with a brief letter dated 29 June explaining why he preferred to send him the article privately. We present here the letter and the final half of his article, which eloquently encapsulates Maragall's position.

AH! BARCELONA...

1 OCTOBER 1909 (PUBLISHED IN LA VEU DE CATALUNYA*)*

When events so grave and so close to home as these strike our spirit, as did the turmoil that took hold in Barcelona during the last week of July, there swells within us a turbulence like that touched off by a great rock plunging from a cliff deep into a small mountain lake: the waters heave and swirl as the sludge stirring in its depths lifts and spreads, clouding it over, and all things aswim are swept amid the chaos, tossing and tumbling, the lightest of them sinking, the heaviest for a moment floating, those at the rim pulled to the center, the centermost flung to the outer edges; until, the sunken rock now stock-still on the bottom, the waters too become quiet and each thing returns to its place as the law of nature would have it, and the waves diminish in rippling circles, clearing as the sediment filters once again to the bottom till the lake lies smooth and still, mirroring once more the pureness of the skies. So it is with our spirit—troubled at such afflictions, it aims to recover its serenity by marshaling unruly passions and jumbled thoughts: fear and anger behind, our skewed judgment rights itself, and hasty resolves are put aside even as the grounding drive that governs our lives moves gently forward, sure of itself, toward that upstanding goal that is its guiding star and will not waver. Then, dispassionately and to good purpose, we can ask ourselves: What is it that has happened? How and why did it happen? What is to be done?

This is where things now stand; nor could the getting there have been rendered any shorter, given the magnitude of the tremor.

First to be unraveled is the pretext, or what seemed the immediate cause of it all. Against the war. Good enough; against a power that forces our sons and fathers from home and takes them off to die for a cause that might be just and noble from the point of view of national or diplomatic imperatives, but which is unpopular, beyond the comprehension of the people, and is to their minds an inexplicable atrocity; and so the people are opposed to it and revolt: better to die in just revolt than to let loved ones die by some decree or to suit someone else's fancy. Good enough, or in any case, understandable. But what has this got to do with arson and desecration and pillaging and insulting and murdering defenseless people, and the destruction of charitable institutions and schools, and inoffensive temples, and bull-headedly prolonging afterwards a state of alarm?

Then comes a second explanation: premeditated revolution hatched by a political party working to their advantage whatsoever state of unrest so as to graft onto it their ideal, or fuel their efforts to do so. But this account comes unraveled as well, since if this were the case, there should have appeared other signs of premeditated action besides burning and sacking: other men would have led the way, other cries would have risen and other workings been set into motion in the revolt. Would you have me believe that the means and aim of any political party would be nothing more than burning convents and posting snipers in windows? I don't think so.

"But," you might object, "this half-baked flop of a revolution and its mobs that took to the streets served precisely those factions whose sole purpose is hatred of the Catholic Church, not to mention those of more rudimentary resolve: hatred pure and simple, and the urge to strike out at others."

This is what H. E. Bishop Torras i Bages has contended in his pastoral: Satan versus God, the Principle of Evil versus Redemption, Hate versus Love. The solution is simple and sublime: embrace the

Cross, suffer the glory of martyrdom, return good for evil, love for hate, overcome merely through example in gentle living, and fortitude in death.

This would have been the long and short of it—no need for another word—and would stand as our serene and overarching objective, should we feel capable of pursuing it. This solution, furthermore, would be far-reaching, the ultimate and definitive grounding of humanity in Christ. But being our timber what it is, if such fortitude were ours, rest assured that it would for the most part have revealed itself quite otherwise. And falling short of exhibiting the valor even to conduct ourselves as men among men, we are accused of lacking the courage of saints among devils. With all due respect to saintly deportment (who can say whether one day within humanity's reach?) we would do well to begin with the former—for the moment more sorely lacking.

To look at it in the world of the here and now, we might ask ourselves: How is it that such things happen to greater extremes in Barcelona than anywhere else?

Why is it that Barcelona is known everywhere as the "city of bombs," and was recently dubbed "that famously infamous city"? Spare me the prattle about how it's the foreigners who are to blame: greater is the infamy in standing by and doing nothing to stop the evil than in doing the evil. So let's not quibble. This was our doing. But how so?

It is essentially a question of upbringing, and as of now, the police, and therefore, the State, wouldn't it seem? The State especially. If every citizen has to go around being a spy and piling up arms at home to shoot it out with the neighbors or the mobs in the streets, it might be a better bet to go off and live in the Rif; or for whoever wants to earn a living in peace, pack up and move to a more civilized country. It is, then, a matter of administrative governance. It stems, however, from geographical considerations.

It is a fact that social turmoil thrives at certain degrees of latitude, like the orange trees that also thrive and bloom here. The revolutionary spirit is strong, like the wine; the filth of the cities seems to be a by-product of the thermometer; beggars abound like the flies; there is abominable dust and pandemonium—and when you stop to think about it, bombs, cussing, and bad coins all flow from the same fount. Bombs and cussing, in particular, amount to the same thing: a destructive outlet for creative impotence. The angel who wished but was unable to be like God blasphemed; the hater of society who feels too weak to transform it tosses a bomb into the thoroughfare. The feeling is the same: angry impotence.

Now consider our excellence in cussing and bombing more generally, and tell me if you don't see a ray of light—a gloomy one. As for flies, beggars, garbage, dust and pandemonium, we've got more or less what we're entitled to; but bombs and cussing are what we do best.

This is a sign that our illness is impotence: a social impotence, let us call it, that supersedes that of other peoples similar to ours; and it entrenches itself more deeply as the population grows. Witness a great conglomeration of individual energies that has failed to create a social organism proportionate to its mass, poorly patched onto a greater State that is to govern it, while we urgently appeal to that State, as though to a foreign power: give us police, armed forces, laws—and we'll build the schools, for later. Police, repression, schools, laws—all band-aids!

Can no one see that what's lacking is love? A horrible lacking, but true nonetheless. Where there is dissatisfaction with life, it comes out as hate, and satisfaction comes out as egoism: all one and the same thing—a lack of love. Love is the primary social "reason," the regenerator of organisms, and sole source of potency. Without it, all is futile. But how can it be gotten? I'll tell you: in the grief that is to come.

Catalonia, Barcelona, your suffering will be great if you wish to save yourself. You'll have to suffer bombings, mourning, pillaging and burning: war, poverty, humiliation, tears—many tears—until from the depths of your sobbing there leaps the spark that will light up your heart with a kind of love—I can't say what kind exactly, but it's all the same. All love is courage, potency, creation, and social virtue; it alone is the mettle of peoples; and only in suffering can it be found. Whoever has not suffered cannot claim to have loved—and sorry are those who suffer without love. Seek out love in your grief, ah! Barcelona—and those who want no part of it, let them leave. And if in the end everyone has gone, the traveler gazing out at Barcelona, and Catalonia, deserted and desolate, might say: Here there may have been a great population, but there certainly never was a people.

CITY OF PARDON

(SENT BY MARAGALL TO LA VEU DE CATALUNYA ON 10 OCTOBER 1909; REJECTED BY EDITOR-IN-CHIEF ENRIC PRAT DE LA RIBA)

Some fine voices that have risen here, and others that I've heard elsewhere, have convinced me that in Barcelona there is a willingness to love. Still, in all these voices, and in others less willing, half-ironic, there stirs or stands out the following question: Toward whom this love that would redeem our city? My answer: What your heart tells you at every moment. Yet I shudder to think how more than one might reply: It's just that right now my heart tells me nothing.

Does your heart tell you nothing, right now, while people drop to the ground before firing squads at Montjuïc only because the sickness that has taken hold in all of us has showed itself more clearly in them? Does your heart not tell you to go beg forgiveness, on your knees if need be—those most offended among you first—on behalf of these fellow citizens now fallen from our grace who out of spite would have torn down the very city we handed over to them in our self-conceit? So that settles it then—they are to pay the price because their actions fall under a code of law, while our inaction is so low that it falls under none at all? To ask that they be pardoned by human justice is to ask that you yourselves be pardoned by justice divine, before which you may well be more guilty than they are.

How can you sit comfortably at home and go calmly about your business knowing that one sunshiny morning, up at Montjuïc Castle, a man will be led out, his hands tied, and brought before all the world, the sky and the sea and the harbor astir, and the dull city rousing itself, and slowly, very slowly, so that he won't have to wait, he'll be taken to a spot in the dried-up moat, and there, when the hour strikes, this man, this magnificent work of God in body and spirit—alive with all his might and all his senses, and the same lust for life in him as in you—will kneel facing a wall, and four bullets will be put in his head, and he'll jump and then drop, dead as a rabbit … this person, once a man, as much a man as you … or perhaps even more a man than you?

How can you sit there at home, your children around you at dinner, and settle into bed with your wife, and carry on with your business, without this vision flashing in front of you and making you choke on your bread as you swallow, or chilling your lips at a loved one's kiss, or keeping you from doing anything else at all?

And this doesn't awaken the love inside you? And still you ask what the object of that love might be, right here and now? What else could it be? How could you possibly think of anything else in the world right now? And how could you have let precious time slip away, while three men have already met their deaths, and how many more to come?

Can you not feel your brotherhood with these unhappy men? Put aside what they've done. Look into their eyes and what do you see? Yourselves. A man like yourselves: no more, no less. I'm not saying he should be set free, scot-free to indulge in his hatred and commit more crimes. No—he, and all the rest of us, we all need to be confined in one way or another, and set straight, even if it means hammering and reshaping from scratch everyone for the love of the new city to come—even if it comes at the cost of great suffering, his and ours, as long as we all suffer together. But kill him? Kill him cold-bloodedly as part of a procedure, at a fixed hour, as if human justice were something certain and infallible, as definitive as the death now being dished out? Is that how it should be?

If you had confronted and killed this man in lethal combat at a barricade in the streets, or at the entrance to a church, I wouldn't blame you. Engaged in such combat, you would have given proof of your love for something, risking your life for an ideal: for the courageous love of an ideal many wrongs may be absolved. But who may absolve you now? Where is your ideal, your love, your sacrifice? Where have you shown your courage? Do not fall into cowardliness a second time. If you failed to show your courage in combat during the struggle, then it's high time you showed it now, in pardoning.

See for yourselves. The lives you will have saved will seem like works of your own; these men, whom you will have snatched from death's door, you will cherish as your own sons; you'll never lose sight of them, and wherever you are you'll care for them, and those like them, and through your love, they, too, will turn to love; and by this act of pardoning that you begin, Barcelona will begin to be a city. No longer will those who hear of this abroad be able to say: "So-and-so was saved by so-and-so because he was black, or white, or red." Instead, they will say: "Barcelona has asked for and obtained pardon for those of hers who were condemned to death." Then, no matter how many bombs there might be afterwards, Barcelona will no longer be the "city of bombs." Instead, her moniker will come from something more powerful than all the bombs and hatred and human malice piled up altogether. Her moniker will come from love, and Barcelona will be known as the "City of Pardon," and from that moment she will begin to be a city.

So let's begin. To the King who holds the power of pardon, to his ministers who may advise him, to the judges who may temper justice with clemency: Pardon for Barcelona's condemned to death! Charity for one and all!

And what a sight it would be to see those most offended the first to begin.

THE CHURCH AFTER BURNING
18 DECEMBER 1909 (PUBLISHED IN LA VEU DE CATALUNYA*)*

I'd never heard a Mass like that one—the arching roof of the church gashed, its walls blackened and broken, its altars destroyed, gone, especially the great dark emptiness where the main altar once presided, the rafters invisible behind the dust from the rubble, no pews to sit on, and everyone standing or kneeling before a wooden table displaying the Holy Christ, and a stream of sunlight coming in through the gash in the roof, along with an army of flies dancing in the stark daylight flooding the church and making it seem like we were hearing Mass out in the streets. The sun poured down on the wooden table where the priest officiated in threadbare vestments, while in the choir, devoid of banister, others sang pressed close to the walls to keep from falling forward.

I'd never heard a Mass like that one. The Holy Sacrifice was there, in life and blood, as if Christ had come to die for men once more, giving up again his body and blood in the bread and wine. The bread and wine seemed freshly made: the host seemed to pulsate with life, and the wine, catching the sunlight as it poured into the chalice, seemed like blood. I'd never heard a Mass like that one.

Everyone who was there, I am certain, before the Holy Sacrifice celebrated at the sparse plain wooden table, before the ill-treated figure of Christ—the table's only adornment—among the dust and the rubble and the wind and the sun sweeping through, and sensing all around us, even now, the lingering destruction and blasphemy that so recently had carried on the same air as the Holy Sacrifice now again—we all heard it as never before, piercing us with new and present-day virtue, as only the Early Christians could have felt, hidden from their pursuers in some secluded chamber of the catacombs, all the more fervent amid the danger and repression of their initiation into the redeeming Mystery.

Then it hit me—the thought, the feeling, that this is how Mass should always be heard; and it seemed to me that afterwards—turning to face the people still coming in through the doorless entrance and passers-by halting, astonished to see the Holy Mystery celebrated out in the open—the priest raised his voice to the gathering crowd:

"Come in! The doors are wide open! You yourselves have flung them back with fire and iron and hate, and here inside you'll find the greatest of mysteries. Love that lives again. By destroying the church you have restored the Church, for this is the true and living Church, the one that was established for you, the poor, the oppressed, the desperate, the hateful. And while it was shut before—opulent within, guarded by the rich and powerful and those who came to put their hearts to sleep in the peace of its shadows—you, with your poverty and your rebellion and your desperation and your hatred, have assailed the doors and opened a breach in her tall walls, and have won her back again. And by your persecution you have returned to us, her ministers, our ancient dignity; and by your blasphemy renewed the strength in our words; and to the Mystery of the Blood you have returned its nearly forgotten virtue through the new blood that has been shed in the turmoil. What a strange thing! Fire has rebuilt, blasphemy has cleansed, and hatred of Christ has reinstated Christ in his house. So come in! Here you will find Him as you have not known Him before, as He is in life and truth, as He wishes to be known by all, especially you."

How stunned and speechess they all would have been if the priest had suddenly turned and said these words! Yet somehow he did, or in any event these words floated on the air in that church after burning, because I heard them, although I don't know how, but I know they rang out inside me, ear-splitting. So when at the sacred moment the priest lifted the host and the chalice before the people, the presence of Christ was so strong and so alive in my heart that I'm unable to describe it. I'd never heard a Mass like that one. In fact, next to that one, I'd never heard Mass at all. Nor do we really realize what Mass is at all; perhaps the majority of Christians leave this world without ever having known Christ. And on top of it all, it takes these people to show us how to get to know Him.

Yes, now I see. The Church lives by dint of persecution—because that is how she was born; and her greatest peril is to be at peace. For this reason, when they see her high-handed, the people instinctively persecute her to restore her to her essential state. So spoke Christ to his ever-persecuted disciples: when not hunted by the powerful, they will be hunted by the wretched, who without realizing it, would return the Church to her natural state.

It is the law of love. Suffering to avoid slumbering, adversity to spark action, oppression to touch off an eruption. The multitude feels more instinctively this law, like all natural laws, and obeys without realizing it—blindly—and their atrocities are none other than this desire gone wild over a thousand paths in darkness, seeking the opening to the light.

You will surely have been struck by a certain resemblance between antisocial cults and the Early Christian Church. Both hold up as their ideal a more perfect state of humanity; in the name of which they detest those who have grown content with the established order, and go about their work above all among the poor, the ignorant and the desperate, and whose apostles and followers have learned to die, when necessary, with all the peace of mind and joy of martyrs.

Whence this faith and courage? Have you never wondered, even as you condemn them? Would you show that kind of courage in defending your faith? And yours ought to be greater since your faith is in Christ, and therefore true and firm faith, while their ideal fades in comparison. What is happening here?

It's simple. Their faith, though it lacks light, is a living faith, while yours, for all the centuries its light has poured from the skies, is a dead one. What do you do to uphold your faith? What do they do? You profess it mechanically, routinely, complying with a few outward practices that neither fatigue you nor place you in danger. They practice theirs with great effort, willing to risk even their lives for it. So what good to you is the light if you've gone blind? Yet their eyes are so sharp that a single thread of gleaming justice filtering through the gloom that envelops them is enough to illuminate them in life and death in a way your own eyes are incapable of seeing. They are chaos striving to shine in the light; while the light shines on you without result, and dies within you, since you have lost your translucence and your glow and you cannot catch it and shine it back out again. If Christ were to walk again among men, surely those to count themselves among his followers would be they, not you.

But now they can't see Christ, so they strike out against his Church, that is to say, against your church. Why? Because they feel estranged among you, and because it is all too peaceful, too orderly, too cut and dried. Their hearts—tormented by ignorance, poverty, and the impotence of their desire—do not seek peace but war, not order but disorder, not the cut and dried but the fresh and innovative. This is why they have created, after a fashion, their own church. Since they see the Church of Christ overrun with things peaceful, orderly, and stale, they raise another one without Christ: chaotic, persecuted, and filled with torment—but full of hope. This is their church, the one that fits them like a glove, the one that their restless faith needs, a living one. Faith slumbers amid tranquillity, and eventually dies. This is why Saint Paul said that of faith, hope and charity, the greatest is charity; and Christ's last and greatest commandment was to love. Love cannot be tranquilized, and only love can keep the other virtues awake and alive: without it, they amount to nothing.

This is what is wrong with you: you seek peace and tranquillity in Christ's Church, you enter without love, you slumber, and you are putting faith to death!

Think about it. What do you ask of Christ when you go to church? You go at fixed hours, you shuffle in through the doorway seeking only tranquillity beneath its vault (that is, if you don't go just for show), forgetting your business and your worries, far from burdens, or else to enjoy your leisure, indulge your lethargy in the easy majesty of sacred music and fragrant clouds of incense, and sleep. And what do you ask of Christ, that is, if you still have the vim and vigor to ask him anything at all? You ask for peace, tranquillity, and oblivion—that he keep you far from trials and bitterness, free you from remorse, and bring you sweet sleep.

This is not Christ's peace. "My peace I give to you, my peace I leave with you." This "my peace" of Christ's is not the peace of this world, which is a world at war. Yet you would establish the Church in a world at peace, so it's no wonder that others, seeing how things stand, raise a cry of war. For them, there is too much tranquillity in your church, too much gloom and sorrow, too many standstill, petrified saints, your song too sluggish, your words of life too hazy— all of which troubles them, and so they rebel and fill the temple with shouting and blasphemy, driving out the drowsy congregation in terror, insulting and sacrificing the ministers at the altar, and they knock down the altar and break the stone saints and burn the church till it topples. Then the church—hunted, assaulted and smoking, stained with blood and blasphemy, empty of song and peace in the world, devoid of doors, altars, walls and vault, and filled with wind and sun and dust and flies, and suffering—once again becomes for them the Church of Christ who died on the Cross.

Don't take it away from them again by building it back with thicker walls, a sturdier top, iron-reinforced doors—these are not its strongest defense, and would only put you back to sleep. Nor ask the State to protect her all the more; it already seemed somehow an official bureau in the eyes of the people. Nor go collecting much money from the rich to raise her up again; unless you want the poor to think she belongs to the wealthy and turn wary of her benefits. Let them be the ones to rebuild it, if they wish. That way, she will be theirs, and only then will they take her into their hearts.

You think that's something they'll never do? Let them see her like she is now: charred, fallen and wretched; abandoned by the rich, who take no comfort in her now, and abandoned by the State, who guarded her in self-interest, or at times relunctantly. Keep on gathering in her: simply and stubbornly—despite the wretched desolation and in defiance of the sun and the cold and the poverty. Let them see you suffering and dying with the sacred bread in your hands. Then the poor will come, rest assured; perhaps in scorn at first, but then with curiosity, interest and admiration. And once they're there, speak the Holy Word to them plainly, so that it rings clear in their ears, just as it was spoken for other ears like theirs; and give them the Eucharistic bread and wine in a simple manner, just as the Lord must have done, and use his same words. Then it will be the poor who rebuild the chuch, you can be sure.

It always seemed to me that what weakened the Church was not enough spreading of the Holy Word. I am not one of her doctors, and I cannot say why things are done the way they are, nor could I say exactly how things might be done otherwise. Still, when I see the way most people act in the temple, the way they hear Mass, their passivity before the huge energy of Christ's loving sacrifice celebrated at the altar, their ignorance of the sublime words that are spoken, and the ensuing distraction or boredom that dazes them as they stand before the most powerful and compelling event in this or the other world, I can only think to myself: "My God! What a sublime treasure gone to waste!" The altar rail appears to be a fortress wall blocking even the tiniest spark of holy fire, the faintest glimpse of shining light from the altar's Holy Mystery burning bright. Everything done and spoken for the people's redemption, for the edification of their souls, happens beyond the altar rail, far from the people, out of feeling's reach, mute to the soul. Of course, Christians are supposed to know what's happening, having been taught at some point, and are expected to fully embrace everything the priest says, either to himself or out loud (though always in Latin and poorly understood by most). Yet I still sense that people have forgotten those teachings of years ago, that they have only an inkling of what is going on, and that truly embracing the priest's words and actions is impossible without an ongoing stimulus, constantly renewed and requiring a spiritual finesse or mystic fervor not to be found in any but the most rare and select of souls; nor do the prayer books made available to the congregation (those who can read) amount to much help—often distracting them or putting them to sleep.

On the other hand, I'm inclined to think that if the priest read out the opening psalms loudly and clearly, and the congregation replied out loud in their natural language; and if the fiery words of the Epistles of Saint Paul rang out, addressed as they are to all men and women throughout the ages; if the Gospel were proclaimed each day in all the divine simplicity of its passages; if the priest offered the bloodless sacrifice for the faithful in a way they could feel it; if he held up the bread and the wine with trembling hands, making everyone else tremble with the measureless meaning of the words that turn them into the body and blood of God, and everyone consummated the sacrifice together, and the Holy Communion were a communion in the full sense of the word—then I am certain that people would not be sleeping or daydreaming. I'm certain that that hour would be for each person the most powerful spiritual activity of the day or week, and that "churchgoers" would be entirely different from what they are now, and that many who have "stopped" going to church would still be going, and would always be going, and Christ's reign among men would surely be otherwise.

Now they've burned down your church. Forgive them, for never was it more true that *They know not what they do*, and not knowing, they cannot take all the blame. So let them know. The doctors of the Church will say how—but let them know; and now that they've defiled your holy place with fire and iron and blasphemy, don't close it up again. Call them into it just as they have flung it open: filling it with rubble and blood and suffering. Don't rebuild the rubble, don't wipe away the blood, don't salve the suffering. What better way to attract those living in suffering and discontent? We would do well to keep in mind the ambivalence in the word "sorry": denoting, on the one hand, those we may regard as deplorable or pitiful, but denoting also those who suffer from grief and sorrow.

FROM MARAGALL'S LETTERS
TO MIGUEL DE UNAMUNO

BARCELONA, 6 NOVEMBER 1902

Sr. D. Miguel de Unamuno,

My dear friend,

Seeing a letter from you is always a happy occasion. Even before reading, I know that I am going to take something good away from it. You are the most living spirit that I know of in Spain. Soul that you are, you bring new life to everything that you touch (your Cartagena speech contains rich and unforgettable remarks on regionalism); in other words, your touch rejuvenates, tapping the eternal youth that is the divinity in things. For this reason I am eager for your letters, second only to meeting face to face, which is always best.

I send you my article on [your novel] *Amor y pedagogía*. I wrote what I gleaned from it, as it is an uncanny book and inexhaustible in meaning. I am usually averse to mixing the artistic with the philosophical, which results in something of a hybrid. Still, it is a work of our times! How else to explain Wagnerian fanaticism? What a great, pedantic and unkindly talent is Wagner's! I believe only in pure art—the people's; no trickery there. The philosophy, the tendency, the thesis in pure art is seen in the state in which the soul is left by it. Nothing more. Great are the theses in the *Iliad* and the *Romancero*. I have just spent a brief sojourn in the heart of our *muntanya*, the mountains of Montseny, far from any town, in a country house, walking on grass, looking up at the sky and hearing the Catalan songs at the living source. Ah! my friend, I have come back happy! I feel all the strength of the *excelsior*! What are Plato's *Dialogues* in comparison? A book.

They did not go so far as to put me in jail for my article "La patria nueva" (The New Country) because the *Diario de Barcelona* is a respectable institution here. They gave me a trumped up trial and then dismissed the case. Our delirium of grandeur is correlate to the State's delirium of persecution; its agents here have stated that they are willing to put up with anarchism (in the wrong sense of the word) but not Catalanism. And so it goes: they see separatism everywhere, and that is the worst of signs. Spain is losing everything, and so will lose herself. She feels persecuted by her own movements of life, and will not rest until dead.

I caught glimpses of Domènech and Robert in your book. Domènech is violent, agressive, like a child, bitter (though not greedy), and above all irritable; but he is not a bad person and he is a man of talent. In Doctor Robert the writer and the thinker were less important; his great quality was his personal charm: with that alone he did more for Catalanism than all the rest. You could say that is how he cured his patients: the great physician with the most vital of qualities!

The matter of your next novel delights me, which I await all the more eagerly since you have seen something of the story yourself. In any event, when it comes to your works I will not enter into discussions about genres or theories of art—something about them grips me and I give in. They are somehow superior to theories.

I see that there is no stopping your restless spirit. The wide spectrum of your studies frightens and attracts me. What a singular man you are! When you say you like my verses and that you translate into another speech the poetry you find in them, I feel proud and flattered.

Do not forget me in your correspondence. I balk at asking you for frequent letters because I understand that you must do what is best for your spirit and for Spain's. Still, do not forget me. Ever and affectionately yours.

Juan Maragall

§

Sr. D. Miguel de Unamuno,
My dear friend,

It gave me great delight to see your letter after so much time. I too believe that humankind should engage in communication no more than in obedience with the rhythm of our hearts—the only way to do so with effectiveness. You tell me that you feel alone, yet how could it be otherwise? Yours is a profound and unique vision of the Castilian reality, so I would think you must live like a prophet out of Israel face-to-face with God and nothing else: in your company others would gain nothing, and it would be your loss. I like and admire that in your noble and strict solitude you are able to see and say the truths that, were it not for standing alone, you could not see or say. Now it is yours that is the inspired and strident voice in the desert, heard from afar, disobedient, but penetrating and purifying. Blessed be such solitude! Your reaction against vulgarity and cut-rate Europeanism is one of the few riches left nowadays in Spain, the only accumulator of spiritual wealth that the people have, the only living reality to be found today in the plains of Castile.

Things being what they are, and you being perfectly aware of it all, how can you bring yourself to go to the theater? It is not your people you will find there, only the public, and it is not the same thing: you will scandalize them to no effect. Each one of them reads what you write in their own home, and every individual soul, alone and pure, is moved by your words; but in the theater there is the beastlike soul of the masses, greedy only for action, impenetrable to words. The mad lover of the dead queen, sublime in what you tell me of him, will die in the theater in vain. You will see. As for [Francis de Sales's] *Treatise on the Love of God*, I have prepared a volume for the Ollendorf library edited by Ors, to which I believe you are going to contribute as well. My new book of poetry is taking shape and I write little for the newspapers. Recently (about two weeks ago) I published an article, "L'església cremada" ["The Church After Burning"] (in *La Veu*) that scandalized a good many because I justified—according to them—the rebellion in July. If I can get hold of a copy I'll send it to you.

Yes, come to Barcelona without making much noise, please: you will see how here we continue living by the sheer strength of living: the week of July could turn up again here at any moment, but so far it has not. La Solidaritat is disbanded, but remains in potential and will reappear when needed. The being and non-being of these social entities is like that of an individual life: it may live, it may die. Yet why it lives and not dies remains a mystery; and when you think about it, it is just as surprising to find oneself living as it would dying. You say that now you feel a change coming on in your life. How so? You cannot say. Blessed be the not knowing that makes us human beings and is the salt of life. May yours be happy and do glory for Spain in [the new year] 1910.

I haven't forgotten you and admire you always.

Juan Maragall

FROM "THE REAL PRELIMINARY QUESTION" / "LA VER-DADERA CUESTIÓN PREVIA" (REPLY TO JOSÉ ORTEGA Y GASSET)

PRECEDED BY MARAGALL'S LETTER TO J. ORTEGA Y GASSET, 29 JUNE 1910

BARCELONA, 29 JUNE 1910

Sr D. J. Ortega y Gasset,

My Dear Sir,

An article of yours that I came across today has prompted me, nearly forced me, to explain once again in writing my feelings concerning the Catalan question. I started out meaning to write an article, but then my tone turned lyrical and I could see that the result was of no value to the public. However, seeing that you were the source of it, and uninclined to tear it up since I had put something of my soul into it, I felt compelled to send it to you in the hope that, since the public you are not, you would perhaps in the serenity of that noble spirit of yours I have come to know, benefit in some way by reading it. So please find it enclosed here, along with apologies for my importunity, and my trust that you will understand, in view of my spontaneous impulse, the affection that your spirit inspires in your humble servant.

Juan Maragall

§

"The Real Preliminary Question"

[...] Catalanism cannot disappear, so don't get your hopes up. It will have its ups and downs as it has in the past (it was held under for centuries and you see how it's sprung back), with or without elected deputies in the Cortes, La Solidaritat will out whenever the need is there, and will dissolve when not needed, and will return and dissolve a hundred times, and a hundred times you will sing victory against it, and another hundred times you will raise the alarm against it. It will all seem to have ended, and it will all begin again. We will strive on both sides, all of us, to erase our differences, to forget all our grievances and to find a common ideal, the highest of ideals—we will say—that unites us, lays a groundwork, makes us all one thing; but always, always, always, I swear to you, this impulse will rise up again, this force, this living thing, acute, immortal: call it the Celtiberian spirit, the particular temperament, the language, the Mediterranean, the Pyrenees, or the line drawn by the River Ebre—or the line of God. Erase it and it reappears, snuff it out and it sparks back to life, smother it and it will breathe again, change it and it will return to what it was, it will never, never, never die. It is God's line; the particular temperament, the spirit, the language. Do you understand? I tell you this in your language, but again, don't get your hopes up because I think it in my own, and I merely translate. For centuries and centuries I have spoken to you in translation, and yet the language has not died. Here it is. It is as alive and well as Portuguese, just over there; alive and well as Spanish, right there on your lips; not on mine, but only in my pen—for now.

Don't you see the significance? It is like a SIGN in capital letters. There lies a something in common in these languages. Spain. All of Spain. Only our lips are different: we are Catalans, Castilians,

Galician Lusitanians. Do you believe you are capable of changing our lips? You will have to tear them from us. Would we want to smother inside them the fundamental word we hold in common? We would end up mute, for no longer would we possess a soul.

You don't understand? Good gracious! What I wouldn't give for you to understand, to reach an understanding with each other in Castilian, in Catalan, in Galician.

Don't talk to me about whether La Solidaritat Catalana is alive or has died. Don't talk to me about civilization, or culture, or higher common ideals; and don't talk to me, in a word, about Spain, unless you first find me the way to have all of Spain; whole and entire, body and soul, threefold and one, like its speech, and like its spirit that would fly free from the Mediterranean to the Atlantic, without obstacles and without borders, but also—and understand this—with each and every single one of its wings.

NOTES

This poem appeared in the volume published for the poet by his friends on the occasion of his wedding (see headnote). Abrams points out the poem's threefold purpose: prologue to the volume *Poesies* (Poems, 1895), correlate to the volume's epilogue poem "Excelsior," and general prologue to the poet's lifelong poetic production (2010, 21). The eight cinquains are written in fully rhyming heptasyllables *abaab* (*a* feminine, *b* masculine lines). Casals (1998, 91) dates the composition between October 1885 and May 1886.

COURTSHIP BY THE BAY OF BISCAY

In the wedding-gift chapbook *Poesías* (see headnote), the poem's sections had not yet been rearranged, nor brought together under a single title.

> 1-4: The alternately rhyming decasyllables of section one are feminine (that is, with an unstressed, uncounted eleventh syllable), suggesting,

Abrams notes (2010, 34), the "harmonious fluidity" of the ocean.

5-18: Section two features non-rhyming decasyllables (blank verse), all feminine; the prosodic shift signals the poet's turning to address his fiancée directly.

6: Abrams notes how the recurrence of foam throughout the poem suggests the goddess of love and marriage, Aphrodite, born from sea foam, illustrating Maragall's symbolic use of the landscape or, as here, seascape (35).

17-18: Maragall occasionally uses a line of ellipsis points to expressive effect. Here, as Casals suggests, they may refer to his fiancée's response to the question posed in line 17; alternatively, perhaps to lines that the poet has omitted here (1998, 118).

19-38: Section three deploys decasyllables that are feminine at the caesura (that is, with an unstressed, uncounted sixth syllable) variously combined with shorter heptasyllables for an effect that is intimate and conversational; at the same time, a subtle yet powerful lyricism comes through in blending and varying both masculine and feminine lines—of either length—in full rhyme.

39-46: Section four varies feminine o-sounding with masculine a-sounding decasyllables in describing a foamy, pitching sea. Abrams reminds us how Aphrodite often feels thrilled at the sight of lovers (2010, 37).

47-78: Section five—the longest—deploys once again shorter heptasyllables, shifting the rhythm from descriptive to conversational and intimate; Abrams notes how the denouement reconciles and brings together opposing elements, among them the lovers themselves, reflected in the varied and fully rhyming interplay between masculine and feminine lines (2010, 38).

WEDDED

First published as a reply to Sardà's verse dedication to Maragall in the wedding-gift chapbook (see headnote), the poem's ninety decasyllables—all feminine—feature full rhyme, mostly alternating, giving a rhythm that blends the verses together with fluidity, suitably framing the harmony and happiness shared by Joan and Clara. Abrams points out the poem's four parts: the wedding (lines 1-14), their travels through Provence and into Italy (15-38), their sojourn in Florence (39-66), and their return to Barcelona (67-90) (2010, 43-44).

1-4: The first four lines appear in a letter to Josep Soler i Miquel dated 25 February 1892 (see Casals 1998, 123).

8: Temple: Santa Anna de Barcelona, parochial church, originally a twelfth-century monastery, located between Plaça de Catalunya and Carrer de Santa Anna, where Joan Maragall and Clara Noble were married on 27 December 1891.

16: As if a captive: see lines 76-79, and note to line 508, *Count Arnau* (part two), on Maragall's use of "captive" in referring to his wife.

23: Our new life all arranged: the couple had found an apartment on Carrer Roger de Llúria to move into upon their return, when Maragall would again take up his position at *Diario de Barcelona*; no less importantly, he was now recognized as a poet of talent by his literary peers (see headnote). Abrams refers to this poem as Maragall's *Vita nuova* (and elaborates on Dante's various influences here and elsewhere (see 2010, 45-46).

43: The great church: the Basilica di San Lorenzo.

47-54: Maragall's poetic rendering of Michelangelo's *David* (1501-1504), housed in the Accademia di Belle Arti. Abrams (2010, 45) remarks on the poet's keen sense of cultural and historical overlay gleaned from the work: ancient Greece (Apollo), Christendom (David as a figure of Christian devotion), the Renaissance (Michelangelo's sculpture), and modern times (tourism).

48: This saint: in the broader sense, since David (c. 1040-973 BCE) predates the Christian era.

55: The cathedral: the Basilica di Santa Maria del Fiore.

57: *Sagrestia*: the New Sacristy, work begun by Michelangelo in 1520, mausoleum for the Medici dynasty in the Basilica di San Lorenzo.

58: *Notte*: *Night* (1526-1531), marble sculpture of a reclining woman by Michelangelo adorning (along with *Day*), the tomb of Giuliano de' Medici, Duke of Nemours (1479-1516).

63-66: Dante supported the White Guelphs, opposing the Black Guelphs, who sought to bring all of Tuscany under the control of Pope Boniface VIII; after Boniface seized Florence with the help of the French prince Charles of Valois in 1301, Dante was condemned to exile from the city. Arno: Major river flowing through Florence.

66-67: Once again Maragall uses a line of ellipsis points to expressive effect (see note to lines 17-18 of "Courtship by the Bay of Biscay"), highlighting the importance of Dante, whose eternal presence closes the section and puts a climactic end to Maragall's sojourn in the city.

69: The relished speech: Maragall's native Catalan.

76-79: see note to line 508, *Count Arnau* (part two), on Maragall's use of "captive" in referring to his wife. And queen still, of the meaning of man: in the wake of the Tragic Week, Maragall would write: "Love is the primary social 'reason,' the regenerator of organisms, and the sole source of potency" (see "Ah! Barcelona..." and corresponding notes in this selection).

86: Clarity (*claror* in Catalan): the reflected meaning connotates his wife Clara (see headnote), whose presence is a source of clarity for the poet.

90: The child on its way: the couple's first child, Helena, was not born until 18 May 1893; the poem's final line may anticipate the biological fact with a statement of intent.

FATHERHOOD

While departing from traditional poetic form and content (see headnote), the poem nevertheless features metered verse (decasyllables, hexasyllables, dodecasyllables, a penultimate octosyllable) and varied end rhyme.

1-4: Maragall refers here to the bomb attack in Barcelona's Liceu Opera House on 7 November 1893 (see headnote).

5-7: Maragall places this attack into the context of previous attacks; the dash at the caesura underscores the separation between attackers and victims.

10: Innocent child: Abrams and Casals have pointed out Nietzsche's influence here (see headnote).

13: Lluís Quintana (2008, 15) has remarked how laughter is in Maragall "the maximum expression of rebellion" here and elsewhere, as for instance in "Song of Return," "Non-Taxable Roses," and "Return."

THE COW GONE BLIND

Among the best known of Maragall's poems (see headnote), its non-rhyming decasyllables, all feminine, occasionally jolt the reader with unconventionally patterned meter, mirroring in form the poem's uncanny content.

1-3: The cow appeared before Maragall and his family on the outskirts of Sant Joan de les Abadesses (see headnote).

4-5: Abrams (2010, 74) notes the irony in stating that the young cowherd's "aim [was] a little too good," since tossing rocks was a herding technique used by the boy, whose overconfidence surpassed his targeting skills.

EXCELSIOR

This epilogue poem, correlate to the prologue poem "Endless Ode" (see headnote), features five quatrains of alternating feminine-masculine rhyming heptasyllables.

1: Keep watch, spirit, keep watch: this initial repetition, epanalepsis, opens the way to numerous repetitions both lexical and syntactic throughout the poem.

13: The standstill land: Maragall depicts the ever-moving sea—in contrast to the unmoving land—to symbolize the vital driving force he is to pursue throughout life (see headnote).

18: Oblivious to: reading, with Casals, *oblidat* (not *oblida't*); see Casals 1998, 195.

THE IMPIOUS HUNTER

Casals (1998, 237) dates the composition of the poem between the appearance of its Catalan-language precedent in January 1895 by Joan Aliberch i Tort and the 1896 Jocs Florals, where Maragall's poem was awarded the Viola d'Or i d'Argent (see headnote).

13: Godhead: the host or consecrated wafer in the celebration of the Eucharist.

15: Devilish: as Moreta (2010, 153) points out, in choosing to chase the hare, symbolizing the Devil, the hunter turns away from God, committing the sin of impiety.

59-64: Stonework torn and tired…: in sharp contrast to the Romantics, Maragall's use of ruins entails not "a nostalgic looking back at the past," but rather a "prophetic looking toward the future [where] buildings of human construction are no obstacle to the expansion of the sacred." (Moreta 2010, 155)

65-66: Not only is the temple no obstacle to the expansion of the sacred (as Moreta notes above), it is not until the temple is destroyed that the Godhead comes into view for the hunter. Similarly, in Maragall's article "The Church After Burning" the partial destruction of the building opens the way to revitalized faith.

FROM *COUNT ARNAU* (PART ONE: COUNT ARNAU) III

With its nearly one thousand lines, the long poem *El comte Arnau* was written and published in three stages over a period of some fourteen years (see headnote). In part one, following the legendary Count Arnau's failed attempt to seduce the abbess (Adalaisa), the "voices of the earth"—conversing with Arnau in the poem as a sort of Greek chorus—mock him for his failure; when he finally succeeds, they shower him with praise; asked what he would wish for, Arnau replies that he would live forever, and so begins his thousand-year scourge, riding through the night, and day, on his flaming horse to the shouts and howls of the voices of the earth. Adalaisa's death ensues, abandoned by Arnau and broken-hearted.

The versification of the poem varies throughout. The sixty-line section included here features quatrains of alternating feminine- and masculine-rhyming decasyllables.

23-32: Moreta (2010, 10, 159) notes the contrast here between religion and sensual beauty (concealed by chaste clothing).

34-42: Moreta (159-160) also notes the contrast between Adalaisa's "heaven" (a personified divinity that would delight in seeing Arnau on his knees) and, conversely, the "heavens" (cosmological spectacle as source of delight for Arnau).

75-78: Moreta (163) notes how Adalaisa's praises of heaven have no effect on Arnau; it is only "the devotion with which the abbess beholds the sacred image [of Christ on the Cross]" that keeps Arnau at bay.

THE END OF SERRALLONGA

Casals (1998, 291) suggests 1899 as the possible date of composition. Maragall's fully rhyming alternating feminine and masculine decasyllables close with a masculine couplet before the poem's four penultimate heptasyllables and reappearance of a single concluding decasyllable whose content flies in the face of the significance of the sacramental ritual just performed (see headnote).

1: Father, forgive me: Serrallonga speaks to his confessor, initiating the sacramental rite of Penance.

9-24: Serrallonga recounts his sins of pride, the first—and often regarded as the worst—of the seven deadly sins; there will follow: wrath (lines 29-44), envy (lines 53-68), greed (lines 73-88), sloth, gluttony and lust (together in lines 93-116).

10, 12: The departure in the Catalan from perfect rhyme here—cos (body) / goig (delight)—underscores perhaps the difficulty of reconciling the body with the demands of the spirit.

13: The king of Spain: Philip IV (r.1621-1665) of the Hapsburg dynasty, under whom Catalonia and Portugal would revolt during the Thirty Years' War; in quelling the Catalan revolt (the Reapers' War, 1640-1652), Philip was forced to neglect Portugal, which regained its independence.

15: He has put our land in strangers' hands: The gradual deployment of Castilian troops throughout Catalonia.

67: Joan Sala i Serrallonga: Serrallonga's real name was Joan Sala i Ferrer; his popular name Serrallonga comes from his marriage in

1618 with Margarida Tallades from Mas Serrallonga de Querós in Sant Hilari Sacalm.

121-138: Joana Massissa was a widow from Castelló d'Empúries with whom Serrallonga lived on the run from 1632 until his capture the following year.

147: This initial line of the final cinquain stands alone in the Catalan as an unrhymed verse ending in "credo," calling attention here to the question of dogmatic faith.

151: 'I believe in the resurrection of the flesh': the eleventh article of faith in the Apostles' Creed (see headnote); preceded in the Catalan by four heptasyllables, this decasyllable closes the final cinquain, set apart from the poem's one hundred forty-six preceding decasyllables.

AT A YOUNG MAN'S DEATH

Elegy composed in October 1895 at the premature death of Maragall's brother-in-law Guillem Noble (see headnote), the poem's two stanzas (6 + 10 lines) feature non-rhyming feminine decasyllables, with the notable exception of a single masculine hexasyllable (line 6).

1-6: In the first stanza the poet speaks to his deceased brother-in-law, praising his athletic, combative vitalism.

6: Casals (1998, 307-308) remarks on the significance of this shorter, rhythm-breaking hexasyllable, bringing the first stanza to its climax in which death itself is experienced to the full (see headnote), and signaling the discursive shift to come in the second stanza where the poet addresses death personified.

7-16: The poet evokes the young man's encounter and final moments with death, his loved ones close by.

7-8: The force of Maragall's irony is strengthened by his personifying direct address and, as Casals notes (308), the familiar tone suggested by the use of the demonstrative *that*.

9-13: Casals (308) notes how enjambment mimics Guillem's irregular breathing and the perturbation of family members standing by.

15: Casals also remarks (308) how this line of monosyllables connotes sobbing.

16: With the reappearance here of the soft, soft sunset from line one, grief seems to be transcended by "contextualizing [the family's] particular loss within the larger cycle of nature and Life with a capital letter" (Abrams 2010, 159).

ASH WEDNESDAY

Dated 1896, the poem is sometimes referred to as "Ash Wednesday: To a young woman" to avoid its being confused with the late poem "Oh Dimecres de Cendra que estens..." (O Ash Wednesday spreading...) composed in February 1911 after the publication of *Seqüències*. The thirteen-line poem's deceptively simple versification features six alexandrines (dodecasyllables, all feminine but one, and all masculine at the caesura but two) and seven hexasyllables (four masculine and three feminine, alternating with respect to the line preceding each one); assonant and full rhyme occur both at line ends and caesuras, with the exception of *sacerdot* (line 7) and *esblaims* (line 13), throwing into relief the contrast here between ecclesiastical ritual and the natural cycle of living (see headnote). Abrams (2010, 165-166) notes the poem's "special sonority, between dramatic and calm, anguished and solemn, forthright and sinuous [where] life prevails" over the constraints of dogmatic faith.

1: Ashes: blessed ashes with which, in the Roman Catholic rite, the priest marks the forehead of the faithful on Ash Wednesday, the first day of Lent.

6-7: The words uttered by the priest while crossing each forehead with ashes are: *Memento homo, quia pulvis es et in pulverem reverteris* (Remember, man, that you are dust and to dust you will return).

13: The Catalan *esblaim* (literally, *act of turning pale*), occurring here in the plural, has been rendered into English as *palettes*, a partial semantic overlap in the sense of "changing color" since, as Moreta notes, "it is a question of colors: the 'young woman' must not renounce the rosy color of her flesh [and] if she does lose it, [it should not be] for having denied or repressed it [...] but for having lived [life's emotions] to the full" (2010, 14).

SONG TO THE CATALAN FLAG

Composed and put to music in 1896, this remarkable poem is widely known as the anthem to the Catalan flag (see headnote). The three six-line stanzas feature alternating masculine and feminine heptasyllables with full intermittent end rhyme, with the additional constraint that all end rhymes throughout the poem feature *a-* or *e*-sounding vowels initially occurring in the three-line refrain; exceptionally, *Senyera* (*flag*) in unpaired line 2 stands out (as a flag well should!) forming only assonant rhyme, not full rhyme, with lines 4, 6 and 8.

1-3: When sung as an anthem, this refrain precedes and follows each six-line stanza.

2: Senyera: the capital letter here indicates not personification, but rather culture-specific symbolic identity, that is, the particular flag in question—the Catalan flag.

16-21: All rhymes, feminine and masculine, feature *a*-sounding vowels in this stanza, standing in complementary contrast to the unpaired second line of the poem that ends with *Senyera* (see the introductory note to this poem above).

NOVEMBER SONG

Casals (1998, 365) remarks on the relationship between "At a Young Man's Death" and "November Song," both dated 1895: "The 'soft, soft sunset' that in October [...] was perhaps the only balsam to ease the suffering caused by death has now given way, in November, to a hedonistic invitation to life without mitigation."

1-6: The first stanza's two non-rhyming feminine pentasyllables (lines 1 and 3) heighten the emotive contrast between autumn and spring, yet blend with and herald (with their *a*- and *e*-sounding vowels, respectively) the longer, fully rhyming masculine decasyllables—the last one paired with a striking masculine pentasyllable topping off the stanza.

7-10: The *a*- and *e*-sounding end-vowel rhyme continues, now inverted, through these four alternating feminine/masculine decasyllables.

11-15: The hard-hitting dictum at the poem's core is compressed into a mere tetrasyllable (line 11), unpaired yet tacking into the shifting rhythm of the following four lines, where feminine heptasyllables (in sharper contrast to line 11 than pentasyllables would be) now alternate with masculine decasyllables, their *i*- and *a*-sounding end vowels throwing line 11 into further relief. Spearheading this masterful form-content synthesis is the leap from the discursive rapprochement of the first-person plural to the bold one-on-one imperative of *Gosa el moment* (Dare the moment)—the poem's *carpe diem* itself taking hold of the poem and infusing it with life.

16-19: A Catalan alexandrine (in this case, a feminine dodecasyllable masculine at the caesura) steers the poem stately toward its conclusion, pairing itself into the subsequent alternating masculine/feminine decasyllables and forming a sub-quatrain with two imperatives that negate life's negation (lines 16 and 17) and an epigrammatic finale that affirms life by way of counterexposition (lines 18-19). Rhythmic and thematic conclusiveness is further enhanced by *e*-sounding end vowels in the last four lines, retrieving and repowering the force of the poem's central dictum (line 11).

THE GOOD-BYES

"Els adéus" (1896) is this first poem of the trilogy that would come to be known as *Els tres cants de la guerra*. In it Maragall adapts to his purpose details of the Biblical account of Cain, poeticizing the separation of young men from their homes and families to act as agents of violence (see headnote). Casals (1998, 373) has noted the literary utilization of Cain by Maragall's Romantic predecessors: Lord Byron's *Cain: A Mystery* (1821), Charles Marie Leconte de Lisle's "Qaïn" (1872), and Victor Hugo's "La conscience" in *La Légende des siècles (première série)* (1859). Maragall uses *vers libéré* here, varying the lines in length, one or more of which are unrhymed in each of the poem's three irregular stanzas.

4: Casals (1998, 376) notes: "Some of the ships that sailed from Catalan harbors did not even reach their destination owing to excessive weight […] not in arms or munitions but in men."

6: Twisting and wailing (Cat. *retorcent-se i bramant*): Both Casals (377) and Abrams (2010, 211-212) note how Maragall's lexical choice in describing the sea-swells prefigures the war awaiting the young men on distant shores.

7-18: In contrast to the Biblical account (Genesis 4:1-17), Maragall's appropriation of Cain entails separation from his wife and children, paralleling that of the conscripted young men.

13: According to the Biblical account, Cain "settled in the land of Nod, east of Eden" (Gn 4:16) (NRSV). Byron's Romantic account concurs: "Eastward from Eden we will take our way" (Byron 182, 27); still, a westerly reference occurs in Byron when Cain tells of his sister/wife Adah's beauty, unmatched by: "The hues of twilight—the sun's gorgeous coming— / His setting indescribable, which fills / My eyes with pleasant tears as I behold / Him sink, and feel my heart float softly with him / Along that western paradise of clouds—" (46). In any case, Cain's poetic westward departure in Maragall coincides with that of the conscripts crossing the Atlantic to the Antilles.

ODE TO SPAIN

Completed on 6 July 1898, "Oda a Espanya" appeared in the
biweekly literary magazine *Catalònia*—number 9, dated 30 June
1898, but published subsequently; Casals (1998, 382) suggests
that the editors delayed publication in anticipation of Maragall's
poem—only days after the Battle of Santiago de Cuba had all but
destroyed the Spanish Caribbean fleet. The poem's strength stems
largely from its form—dramatic monologue (as in "The End of
Serrallonga")—in which the poet's voice captures and conveys poignantly the deontological rift separating Mother Spain's perception
of herself and her culturally distinct children's perception of her. A
decade later, in his 1908 article *Visca Espanya!* (Long Live Spain!)
Maragall would argue forcefully from a similar vitalistic framework
for linguistic and cultural pluralism throughout Spain: "[Spain] must
live in the liberty of its peoples; each free in itself, drawing, from its
own soil, its own soul; and from its own soul its own government,
so that together they may remake a living Spain, governing itself
freely and of itself. This is how Spain must live. Long live Spain!"
(Maragall 1960, 767). The forty-two line poem unfolds in eight
cinquains—except for the first and fourth stanzas, which are sex-
tains—of mostly octosyllables feminine at the caesura, each stanza featuring non-rhyming first and second verses, masculine and
feminine respectively, and a masculine-rhyming couplet preceding
a final half-length feminine tetrasyllable, varying in the two penultimate stanzas (see below, notes to lines 32, 36-37 and 38-42).

2: A language that isn't Spanish: Catalan.

7: Saguntians: the colorful history of the town of Sagunt (Sp. Sagunto)—

from the ancient Celtiberian settlement to Roman (Saguntum) and Carthaginian occupation, and from Muslim Spain to the Reconquista—acquires added ideological significance in the telling of Spanish history from the fifteenth century onward, starting with the Castilian Trastámara dynasty ruling in Valencia as a result of the Battle of Morvedre (Sagunt) in 1412. Spanish militarism—which Maragall targets in the poem— asserts itself again in Sagunt in 1874 when General Arsenio Martínez Campos led the military uprising against the First Spanish Republic.

8-11: Mother Spain's notion of patriotic self-sacrifice estranges her from the joy of living.

23-32: Abrams (2010, 217-218) notes how the fifth and sixth stanzas allude clearly to the fateful departure and fatal outcome described, respectively, in "Els Adéus" and "Cant del retorn."

29: The poem's first decasyllable in the original Catalan spotlights the fatal outcome of the military expedition.

32: The poet/child's moving entreaty stands out as a hexasyllable in the original Catalan; all other stanzas end with a shorter tetrasyllable.

36-37: The stanza-ending pattern is inverted here with the shorter tetrasyllable preceding the stanza's final line. And smile at the sevenfold colors arching the clouds: The poem's second decasyllable in the original Catalan stands out all the more as the penultimate stanza's final line, entreating Mother Spain to embrace and delight in her own rainbowlike multiple identity.

38-42: The poem's final stanza might be likened to a symphonic finale, with the poem's third and finally fourth decasyllables (lines 39 and 41) framing between them the poem's sole dodecasyllable (line 40) and forming a maestoso triad building up to the climactic *adagio-risoluto* concluding line, *Adéu Espanya*.

SONG OF RETURN

Dated 1899 and written in a "political and social atmosphere charged with tension" (Casals 1998, 385), the poem precedes an article published the following year in *Diario de Barcelona* (Maragall 1900) in which Maragall favorably assesses the book *La Escuadra del Almirante Cervera*, written by Admiral Víctor Concas i Palau (1845-1916), whose first-hand account of the Battle of Santiago de Cuba left little doubt as to the folly of the naval undertaking. Maragall would write: "Spain sleeps, she has been sleeping for a long time. At times it does not appear so because she moves, but she moves unconsciously in a heavy torpor, inexpugnable like that which often sets in before death" (Maragall 1961, 594). Only the first and fifth of the poem's six stanzas vary from the basic sextain pattern (see notes to lines 5 and 26-29 below), which features fully rhyming alternating feminine and masculine decasyllables, all feminine at the caesura; the first, second and fourth stanzas feature a half-length pentasyllable, forming a rhyming pair or triplet with preceding feminine or masculine decasyllables. The rhythmic effect might be said to suggest a military drum dirge (which we have attempted to re-create in English translation using a basic decasyllabic and pentasyllabic meter as well), conveying and sustaining the mournful tone throughout the poem until its dramatic upturn at the end.

4: The original Catalan features a half-length pentasyllable here, as do lines 11 and 23.

5: With nothing but sharks and dolphins in tow: this is the first stanza's additional line. Sharks: Casals (1998, 387) notes the intertextual allusion to Aeschylus (see headnote). In tow: Naval victors often towed their captured vessels behind.

26-29: Signaling the concluding upturn, the poem's sole quatrain omits the recurring couplet with its final chantlike tetrasyllable *ploreu, ploreu* (let go your tears) common to all previous stanzas. Our country: In contrast to line 8 in "Oda a Espanya," *la pàtria* refers here to the Catalan homeland. The words (Cat. *la llengua*): the Catalan language.

30: Shoring up the people's collective life, in addition to the language, is the "memory of other deeds" or commonly shared history that, as Abrams points out (2010, 221), stands in stark contrast to Spain's memory/history in "Oda a Espanya."

31-33: Alongside the shared language and shared history particular to the human geography, the symbolic force of the natural geography is climactically foregrounded: "the marching peaks" and "forests" represent what Torrents (2003, 245) has pointed out as the telluric or geographic element of the Catalan homeland; among several mountain ranges that have been strikingly poetized for their historic and symbolic significance, it is the Pyrenees, and most especially, Mount Canigó, that—thanks to the foundational epic poem *Canigó* (1886) by Maragall's predecessor Jacint Verdaguer (1845-1902)—looms largest in the Catalan literary system.

34-35: The poem's remarkable turnaround is punctuated by the reintroduction of the solemn salutation (line 34) previously occurring in all stanzas but the penultimate; now, however, heartened by the hope that the threefold legacy evoked in the preceding lines (language, memory and land) lives on, the poet breaks the spell of the dirgelike verse with an astonishing final heptasyllable, redirecting the poem's rhythmic force toward a compelling shift from dark to light, from tears to laughter and song, the revitalization of the poem itself prompting the revitalization of the people.

AT PLAY

The poem's rhyming heptasyllables begin as couplets (lines 1-6), with a feminine triplet separating lines 7 and 11, whose final masculine rhyme recalls the sole masculine couplet at the poem's outset. The overall effect is a musicality that mimics the playful "ring-a-ling" of the poem's opening refrain. The poem was put to music by composer Francesc Pujol i Pons (1878-1945).

1-3: Lines 1 and 2 reproduce the opening of a traditional children's song associated with hiding an object, serving as Maragall's point of departure for his poem. Line 3 alludes to a similar game evoked in *Lyrisches Intermezzo* (26) by Heinrich Heine (see headnote to this section).

7-11: With the rhyming pattern of an *abbba* cinquain, the feminine triplet defers the completion of the final couplet in a playful climax, bolstered by the direct-speech response at the tail of the final staggered line "Pel cel" (" 'N heaven"). Undoubtedly, the worldly focus of the final lines and their end rhymes strengthens a metaphoric reading of heaven, with the poet's gaze fixed firmly on earth; the final lines (9-11) allude to Heine's "Ich glaub nicht an den Himmel" ("I don't believe in Heaven").

HOSPITALITIES

Most likely composed in March 1903 (Casals 1998, 479), it is among the latest of the poems in the volume *Les disperses* (1904). Its alternating masculine-feminine heptasyllables, notes Abrams (2010, 261), with assonant *a*-sounding rhyme at feminine lines in two stanzas of different length give the poem the feel of a traditional song, such as one the herder himself might sing.

TITLE: Unlike the original Catalan title, the ambivalence of the English "Hospitalities" is today semantically severed from its etymological root (see headnote to this section).

1-2: This refrain occurs three times throughout the poem, mirroring its repeated utterance by the herder.

5: Bandaged and swollen: the herder is recovering from cataract surgery.

22: That bright refrain anew: amid his inhospitable surroundings, the herder turns to his song for strength and vitality.

25-26: The power of the herder's song lies in its ability to evoke the flowers as if they were physically present—ability which Maragall evokes, and reenacts, through the poem itself. In a variant of the poem (see Casals 1998, 479), there is a four-line envoi which reads: "Jo te les envio amic, / si en tos jardins vols plantar-les / tu ja les sabràs conèixer, / més belles ja no en sé d'altres." (I send them to you friend, / should you want them for your garden / you'll know what to make of them, / I know no others lovelier.)

SUNSTRUCK

Composed in 1899, the poem's form is essentially that of a traditional *codolada*, popular in tone (often found in medieval narrative or satire), alternating decasyllables with, for the most part, shorter hexasyllabes.

1: The partly formulaic beginning, typical of a folktale, sets the discursive tone.

2-3: Casasses (2014, 39-40) notes the simple, generic quality of the young woman's description: her loveliness and her age. Curiously, the Catalan *bella* ("lovely") is structurally spotlighted at the end of line 3, the only unrhymed line in the Catalan poem.

5: That girl is like sunshine: little do these "people from all around" know that the figurative sense of the Catalan idiom com un sol ("like a sun") will soon turn literal (40).

12-13: "Disrobed" and "with relish": Casasses (42) notes the utter absence of sin or guilt in connection with sensual pleasure here.

14: Casasses (43-44) underscores the straightforward, unpretentious speech here, consistent with the folktale-like quality of the poem and strengthening its effectiveness in conveying its uncomplicated human truth.

22: Just as there is no guilt, nor is there any sadness or darkness in the poem (47).

24-31: Maragall provides the reader with the exact content of the song; Casasses (47) notes the connection with the ending of *Count Arnau* (part three), where it is a "young woman's living voice" that brings redemption.

26-28: "Shines," "sparkle" and "redden": Maragall's use of active verbs here endows each part of the body with life (48).

31: Casasses notes that this line is "a central pillar of the poem": "The woman lights up the light [and] the light / has loved her and she carries it within" (49).

35: Strange song: "The song is strange because it is neither of this / world nor the other, but of both: not the heaven and hell / wedded by Blake, but earth and the heavens, / the two paradises" (Casasses 2014, 50).

51: I come to bring the heavens nearer the earth: Casasses (2014) underscores how Maragall "does not say bring together [...] nor that we rise / to heaven to take our places there [...] nor that [the child] has come to save us [...] but only that he wishes / that the distance between the earth and the heavens / be made shorter [...] not / by moving the earth but by moving the heavens" (54-55). Maragall invites us through the poem to engage in a freedom that is vital, not abstract; and to embrace the joy of the young woman and be a "light within the light. Any other policy would lead to hell / and leave us in the dark" (57).

NON-TAXABLE ROSES

Included in a letter to Caterina Albert dated 4 May 1903 (see head-note), the poem has been described as the "work of a goldsmith" (Abrams 2010, 304). Its fully-rhyming masculine decasyllables, all feminine at the caesura with the exception of one (see note to line 2), are topped off with a final, climactic hendecasyllable signaling the completion of the natural life cycle (see note to line 16).

2: Some dark red ones: Abrams (2010, 304) notes how this is the only initial hemistich (in the original Catalan) that is masculine at the caesura, spotlighting the eventuality of death and anticipating the "exceptionality of the final line" (304); the varying colors may suggest the various stages of the life cycle (298).

3: Abrams (2010, 298) notes the shift here from first-person to third-person narrative, strengthening the sense of textual objectivity as Maragall "yields protagonism to the flowers."

5: These roses know no servitude: personification of the roses moves the poem "from physical description to symbolic meaning," where the flowers have the "typically human capacity for self-determination" (Abrams 2010, 298).

7-8: The aim and purpose of these roses is to live their own lives (299).

9-12: Beauty is depicted here as something that cannot be had or possessed: in attempting to contain beauty, "humanity only manages to cut short the life cycle" (299).

13-14: The uncontained beauty of these roses may be appreciated by anyone who is sufficiently alert to notice them.

15: Laugh: Lluís Quintana (2008, 15) has remarked how laughter is in Maragall "the maximum expression of rebellion" here and elsewhere, as for instance in "Fatherhood," "Song of Return," and "Return."

16: The natural closing of the life cycle, free from containment, is rhythmically highlighted here by the metrical shift to a concluding hendecasyllable.

VIEWS OF THE SEA

The various sections of the poem are dated (Maragall 1960, 109–110): I, 5 Apr. / II, 16 Apr. / III, 18 Apr. / IV, 20 Apr. / V, 9 May.

EPIGRAPH: The rhyming heptasyllables describe the traditional Good Friday procession held at night in Caldes d'Estrac. Casals (1998, 618) notes the allusion to Matthew 4:15–17 and Isaiah 9:2, and more particularly, to *Count Arnau* (Part Three, line 109): "They are Sorrow, king of the earth."

1–4: The unrhymed feminine decasyllables flow easily, setting the tone for the reflection on change and permanence suggested in the imagery (see Abrams 2010, 326–328)

5–9: The shift to a colloquial tone marks the relating of an everyday event, throwing into relief the uncanny, transcendent nature of that event. Abrams notes how the calm sea depicted by Maragall clashes with the Gospel accounts, yet remains consistent with the poetic inquiry undertaken here (2010, 329–331). The predominantly feminine decasyllables are offset by two masculine lines (the first and the third), presignaling the shift to prevailing masculine lines in the following section (lines 10–19).

10–19: This lyrical tour de force celebrates the wonder of the sensorial link between self and world, now deploying verses that contract to shorter pentasyllables, their effect heightened by the prevalence of masculine lines—except for lines 12, 14 and 16, ending in *enamora*, *miro* and *juntes*, anticipating the sensorial and emotive communion between self and world culminating in lines 17 through 19.

17–19: The emotive charge ("Make my heart grow wide") is simply yet potently packaged with the post-positioning of the sensory stimuli, whose nominalized colors "the green" and "the blue"—elements of subjective sensory perception—blend, yet stand separately and equally with their objective counterparts in the external world: "the pines" and "the sea."

20–31: The magnitude of the contemplative event in the previous section is now matched by a dynamic event, the forming and breaking of a wave, evoking the "great and unending process of creation and destruction in nature and life in general" (Abrams 2010, 333). The predominance of pentasyllables, now all feminine, mirrors yet inverts the previous section, while the longer hendecasyllables (lines 22 and 31) suggest both the cresting and crashing of the wave and the repetition of the creation–destruction cycle.

32–41: Susanna Rafart notes: "[Maragall] moves toward life […] the moment the boats disappear a very subtle doubt sets in, quickly dissipated by the splendid and skillfully orchestrated return" (Quintana et al. 2008, 41). Terry (1999, 98) notes how the boats, tracing their pathways out at sea, are an allegory for the imagination; nor do they lose their way in the unknown, returning "impregnated with their magic force." Matching the return of the boats, this concluding section returns to decasyllables, offset by a single hexasyllable (line 36), all feminine except for lines 33 and 34, ending in *mar* and *sol*, which in turn resonate in assonant rhyme with the poem's concluding lines ending in *barca* and *olorosa*.

THE MOUNTAINS

Composed in 1901 between 20 July and 17 August in Camprodon (see headnote), this poem has been described by poet and critic Gabriel Ferrater (1922–1972) as "possibly Maragall's lyrical masterpiece" (quoted in Abrams 2010, 338).

1–20: The adroitly crafted quatrains of assonant rhyming heptasyllables open with an initially paired masculine *o*-rhyme (first stanza), substituted by alternating initial pairs of masculine *a*- and *i*-rhymes (stanzas 2–5), with a single recurring masculine *e*-rhyme in the third line of each stanza, and with a recurring *o*-rhyme, now feminine, closing each stanza.

21–38: The initial couplet (lines 21–22) in which the "all" and the "I" merge into one maintains the previous heptasyllabic meter and completes the form–content synthesis with the return to the poem's opening masculine *o*-rhyme, while at the same time blending with the subsequent decasyllabic couplets which take stock of, as Abrams notes, a number of features comprised in the land, water, air and natural life (2010, 342). The poetic statement of the blending of self with the natural world is further enhanced by anaphora (varying slightly in some of the couplets' first lines).

39: This climactic and uncanny nine-syllable verse is the only one to stand alone throughout the poem, marking the moment in which the self merges with the highest feature of the land, "the heights of ranging peaks," and anticipating the fruition of the mind and the senses (to unfold in lines 40 to 54).

40–54: This section's initial tercet (lines 40–42) embraces the previous isolated verse (line 39), forming a disconnected quatrain featuring the only instance of enclosed rhyme (*abba*) in the poem, set apart from yet anticipating the stanzas to follow while at the same time blending with the previous section. The coalescence with nature draws to its climactic conclusion with the treatment of the material–spiritual dichotomy in this section's final lines, "[I] stood sturdily up to carry to the skies / all that was around me and within me," recalling analogous treatment in "The End of Serrallonga," "Spiritual" and, as noted by Abrams (2010, 345), "Sunstruck."

55–58: Preceded by ellipsis points signaling the return to the self separate from the world, the final quatrain of heptasyllables returns, also, in form and content to the initial moments of the encounter. Now, however, the poet/reader carries within the "secrets / of the mysterious earth."

RETURN

The composition of "Retorn" between 9 and 13 September 1901 (just weeks after "Les muntanyes") coincides with Maragall's travels to Gavarnie, Lourdes, Pau, Toulouse, Carcassonne, Elna (Elne) and Olot with friend Víctor Sanpere (see Casals 1998, 633; Moreta 2010, 482). This series poem in five sections features mostly decasyllables and hexasyllables alternating variously in masculine–feminine assonant rhyme.

1–11 (section I): The abundance of antithesis—deep ravines–high skies, flatlands–mountain, black–white, and particularly captive–freedom—underscores the magnitude of the unbridgeable gap suggested here between self and world. The notion of freedom will reappear in the poem's fifth section.

8–9: Where mountain flowers / fragranced my heartfelt longing…: the beauty and wonder of the mountains persist, despite their impenetrability. Casals (1998, 634) notes the use of ellipsis points here after *longing*, revising and substituting specific objects of longing that appear in an earlier version of the poem, suggesting now a more general, existential sense of longing inherent in the human condition.

12–18 (section II): In this short stanza (the poem's shortest section), the impact of the poet's gaze is redoubled by the parallel, personified gaze of the lake. Abrams (2010, 350–352) notes an intertextual allusion to Psalm 137, underscoring the breadth and depth of the poetic statement here.

13–14: Lake: Gaube Lake (see Casals 1998, 634), lying at an altitude of 5660 feet southward from the town of Cauterets. Vignemale: Highest of the French Pyrenean peaks (10,820 ft.), its massif rising to the south of Lake Gaube along the French–Spanish border.

19–27 (section III): A sense of claustrophobia (see Terry 1999, 99–100) precipitates the poet's flight to the flatlands, bringing the *in situ* encounter with the mountains to a close.

19: Gavarnie: Gavarnie Falls, one of Europe's most spectacular waterfalls (1385 ft.) located southeast of the Vignemale massif along the French–Spanish border.

25: Dreaded Pyrenees!: exclamatory apostrophe occurs here for the first time since the poem's opening line, signaling thematic closure and further underscoring the shift to the subsequent encounters in sections four and five.

27: Tarbes: city northeast of Lourdes.

28–45 (section IV): Maragall's visit to Lourdes where some 20,000 pilgrims had gathered is described in detail in his article "Lourdes"

(*Diario de Barcelona*, 3 Oct. 1901), including his impression of the young woman depicted in lines 41–43.

35–36: Like the mountain flowers, the miracle also "blossoms gently," exerting its wonder and beauty in the presence of the faithful.

40: This concise, solitary pentasyllable in the original Catalan encapsulates strikingly the condition of the afflicted in general, powerfully particularized in the example of the young woman in the lines following (41–43).

44–45: Maragall refers here to the evening procession, also described in his article (see note to lines 28–45): "The endless file of pilgrims passed interminably, their lighted candles in their hands, chanting tirelessly."

46–57 (section v): The opening exclamatory apostrophe of this section is in fact twofold, its second utterance extending over three and a half lines (46–49), invoking the fabled past of Béarn, a medieval viscounty whose sovereignty was linked variously over the centuries to the Kingdom of Navarre and the Crown of Aragon, including the Houses of Trastámara, Foix, Albret, and ultimately Bourbon; Henry III of Navarre, by marriage to Margaret of Valois (daughter of Henry II of France), would become Henry IV of France (1589–1610), precipitating France's sixteenth-century religious wars (Henry, a Huguenot until the circumstances of his reign advised conversion to Catholicism, would issue the Edict of Nantes); under the ensuing French dominion, Béarn was ripe for outright annexation by Louis XIII in 1620. Separately, in the fifteenth century, the succession to the Kingdom of Navarre disputed by John II of Aragon triggered the Catalan Civil War (1462–1472), which pitted the independence of Catalan institutions against encroaching royal authority.

47–49: This clear reference (see Casals 1998, 635–636) to the legendary musketeers popularized by Alexandre Dumas (1802–1870) embodies ideals of human action that contrast sharply with the "human flocks" of the previous section (line 30). Land of liberty: Maragall here celebrates the triumph of the elusive freedom that he originally sought in the mountains (section I). Laughter: As elsewhere, occurring in connection with rebellion and freedom (see notes to "Fatherhood," line 13, and "Non-Taxable Roses," line 15).

50–53: Graceful balcony: Casals (636) discusses the problem of establishing the location of the balcony with certainty, pointing out that it might be the Palau dels Reis de Mallorca, in Perpignan, although she seems to weigh in in favor of Pau, the historic capital of Béarn. Pyrenees!: This is the poem's third exclamatory apostrophe invoking the mountains, now from afar, paralleling in spatial distance the invoking of Béarn over the remoteness of time. Like a row of ghosts: Béarn's fabled past may also be construed here as comprised in the mountains' elusive, haunting presence. Sky's blue: Maragall's formulation again nominalizes the color, enhancing its sensorial strength (see note to lines 17–19, "Views of the Sea").

54–55: The poem's concluding exclamatory apostrophe is again twofold (mirroring this section's opening lines), but the apostrophic farewell predicates the poet's "last vision" of the mountains, that is, not the mountains themselves but rather his perception of their image in the mind, suggesting the strength and fecundity of their hold on the collective imaginary.

56–57: The sparing but decisive recurrence of *o*- and *e*-sounding paired verses across the poem's several sections (lines 1–2, 14–15, 44–45, 56–57) in the original Catalan underscores the notion of return, by which the imagination and reflection on key events and impressions spark an ever-rekindling life of the mind with a view to its connection, or disconnection, with the world.

RETAKE

Casals (1998, 639) dates the poem late 1901 or early 1902. Its dignified tone is enhanced by traditional alternating masculine–feminine decasyllables featuring assonant o-sounding rhyme at feminine lines.

1: The opening line repeats the closing line of the previous poem, "Return" (see headnote).

4: My Barcelona: Casals (1998, 638) notes the subjective formulation here, foregrounding the self in relation to place.

5–6: Almond trees / the sea: return to the imagery of the opening poems of *Enllà* (see headnote). Mallorca: Counterpoints the historical, cultural and geographic affinity of Occitan– and Catalan–speaking territories; this is further explored in the fourth and final poem of the cycle *Les muntanyes*: "Glosa" (Ballad; not included in this selection), in which a popular ballad attributed to Gaston III (1331–1391, Count of Foix and Viscount of Béarn) serves Maragall as starting point for this 116–line poem evoking the Pyrenees as a shared historical and cultural crossroads for a "united Pyrenean Romance–language community" (Passola 2012, 338): "Love will appear on the summits, / its rays shining in the blue, / and what once was barrier / will be the kingly seat of union. / Our gentle speech, its tints and hues / reflected a thousand-fold across our kindred valleys, / is understood to all: / with open arms we call each other brothers. / We all descend from the same heights, / drink water from the same snows, / sing songs whose tunes are the same, /

and with our cries come ringing out the same echoes." (See also Casals 1998, 640–647.)

FROM COUNT ARNAU (PART TWO: THE SOUL) SCHOLIUM

Maragall composed the nearly six hundred lines of part two of *El comte Arnau* between 1901 and 1904 (see headnote). Topping off the seven sections preceding it, "Scholium" concludes part two with a conversation between the spirit of the deceased Adalaisa (with child) and the Poet—endowed with both body and spirit—who now through his own creative device makes his entrance into the narrative itself. The Poet leads Adalaisa along a divided path: he in the sunshine, she in the shadows. With its one hundred forty-three lines (part two's longest section), "Scholium" blends, in the original Catalan, an elaborate and forceful versification consisting in the main of fully rhyming alternating masculine and feminine decasyllables and balladic heptasyllables, while strategically varying meter and rhyme to signal a number of consequential moments in the poetic narrative.

452–457: These introductory decasyllables are the narrator's, whose voice will give way to those of Adalaisa and the Poet for the remainder of part two. It is the only stanza featuring all-masculine rhyme. Quintana (1997, 16) has discussed the significance of several elements recalling the first canto of Dante's *Inferno*.

458–467: A single masculine rhyming couplet signals Adalaisa's opening decasyllables, linking them to the previous stanza, yet the subsequent shift in versification marks the entrance of her own voice, which alternates feminine and masculine decasyllables.

463: Adalaisa evokes Arnau here, whose voice (among others) she hears, but it will be the Poet who replies.

467: The dream of eternal restlessness: Adalaisa mocks the poet, whose role and power of imagination are depicted analogously in the closing lines of "Excelsior" ("there is no end in sight, / there's to be no end to your journey") and the opening line of "Views of the Sea" ("the sea forever restless").

468–470: The Poet's entrance into the narrative is signaled by a shift to heptasyllables.

471–483: Adalaisa not only follows suit, shifting also to heptasyllables, but completes the masculine rhyme *dol/sol* in her reply, blending the Poet's voice with hers, and at the same time, throwing into relief the sharp contrast here between *dol* ("suffer") and *sol* ("sun").

471: There's nothing like seeing the sun!: thrown into relief formally (see note above), this striking exclamation gathers force from analogous rejection of the life of the spirit without the life of the body in other Maragall poems, perhaps most notably "The End of Serrallonga" (*Visions & Cants*) and "Spiritual" (*Seqüències*).

484–487: The Poet's retort is one of conformity on two counts: formally, the heptasyllables continue to follow suit, while their content merely reaffirms the Christian doctrine of the resurrection of the body and eternal life; recalling, again, "The End of Serrallonga" and "Spiritual" (see note above).

488–489: It is Adalaisa who makes the bold break with conformity, questioning the Christian doctrine of renouncing the life of the body— paralleling, of course, Maragall's bold poetic statement in "Spiritual" and other poems challenging dogmatic authority and reaffirming the joy of living in the world. The dogmatic break is mirrored by a remarkable prosodic break: an innovative couplet blending an un-canny feminine–masculine near-rhyme—"acontentes" / "tens"—that underscores Adalaisa's challenge to dogmatic authority as the crucial turning point in the poetic dialogue.

490–505: When the Poet's existential contradiction is put to him point blank, his justification for enjoying the privilege of living the life of both body and spirit hinges on his ability to empathize with his fellow-beings ("If I can see in the workings of this world / What is pleasure or is pain for you"); barring this, he is forced to step down from the double life: ("But should this being be pulled apart / And my senses none but bodily, / I'd just as soon be rid of them, / And be, like you, spirit only"). Halfway through the sixteen-line stanza, the Poet's argument shifts to commitments of a more contingent nature: "I have a wife and children" and "from the ancestral mountaintops / Come cries of our renaissance fraught with risk"—in other words, he must answer the call of family and countrymen. Further inscribing reflective force into the Poet's reply to Adalaisa's incisive challenge is the return to decasy-llables (the Poet's first). Finally, once again, the thematic shift halfway through the stanza is signaled by prosodic variance: the stanza begins by breaking the previous pattern with a high-powered all-masculine enclosing rhyme (*abbacddc*)—in which lines *bb* complete Adalaisa's previous masculine heptasyllable—then shifts back midway to alter-nating feminine–masculine rhyme (*ababcdcd*).

501: Come cries of our renaissance fraught with risk: Lluís Solà (2012, 225) stresses the nature and importance of the Catalan renaissance in which Maragall plays an important part: "The struggle between death imposed and life recovered, not only where the [Catalan] language is concerned, is one of the keys to understanding the renaissance movement. [... Maragall] saw the virtues and possibilities in [the Catalan language] and, at the same time, the dangers that continually beset it." Separately, and no less importantly, the line echoes Maragall's invocation of Mother Spain in the closing verses of "Ode to Spain" (*Visions & Cants*).

503: To struggle and to love I need my arms: the Poet's affirmation contrasts with, yet echoes, Arnau's reply to Adalaisa when abandoning her: "Mine only are my arms and footfall" (Part One,IX; see headnote to *Visions & Cants)*.

506–513: Following up on the Poet's remark about his wife and children, Adalaisa queries further into his married life, prodding a response containing heartfelt biographical details given by Maragall ("the Poet") in the subsequent stanza. Adalaisa's decasyllables continue the full feminine–masculine alternating rhyme of the previous stanza, with the added prosodical force of echoing and repeating the previous stanza's final masculine rhyme for a total of six occurrences of identical end rhyme: *b... b // ababcbcb*.

508: And with a captive (*captiva*) wife at home: compare with "Wedded" lines 15-16: "I led her, in the vague night, / from her mother's hearth as if a captive (*presonera)*;" and lines 76-79: "There, the nuptial home awaits / the groom who brings the bride now captive. / Captive (*Captiva*)—only of love: queen sovereign / at a hand's touch of all things; / and queen, still, of the meaning of man." See also note to lines 510-511 below.

510–511: So tell me how you came to find her / And where love bloomed and where it seeded: this is the first in a number of remarkable intertextual elements in connection with Maragall's first encounter with Clara Noble alluding to Catalonia's foundational epic of the Catalan Renaixença, the long poem *Canigó* (1886) by Jacint Verdaguer (1845–1902); preluding the young Gentil's first encounter with Flordeneu, queen of the Pyrenean faeries, one of her subjects alerts the young knight: "You'll see in just what garden blooms and seeds / The flower of loveliness that stirs your dreams" (*Canigó*, II, 131-132). The use of "captive" in the previous line (508) also resonates with the Gentil–Flordeneu encounter in *Canigó*, in which the queen of Pyrenean faeries is no less captive than is Gentil: "A sovereign who, surrendering an empire, / Is slave to him whose love she steals away" (*Canigó*, II, 185-186).

514–539: Maragall employs *vers libéré* here, breaking with the rigorous rhyme patterns of the rest of "Scholium" and spotlighting the inscription here of his own autobiographical footprint in the Poet's reply. Predominantly unrhymed feminine decasyllables, the 26-line section features only five masculine lines.

514–515: High in a Pyrenean valley one summer / I saw her for the first time: it was in the Pyrenees of Puigcerdà that Maragall first saw Clara Noble while sojourning there with his parents and sisters in the summer of 1888; he was twenty-seven, she fifteen years of age (Casals 2011b, 16-17).

516–518: Long I looked before I saw: / Her beauty well concealed: Clara Noble would later write in her memoirs: "It took Maragall one or two days to take notice of me; truth be told, I would hide myself in nooks and crannies where I wouldn't have been seen" (quoted in Casals 2011b, 17). Like balmy violets deep in woods: compare with Verdaguer's "Why lie in hiding, stream-cooled Camprodon, / Violet growing wild along your banks?" (*Canigó*, IV, 25-26).

520: Crimson rose: the French rose or *Rosa gallica* (Cat. *rosa vera*) is frequent in Romantic poetry of the Renaixença; Verdaguer associated it with the Blessed Virgin in his *Llegenda de Montserrat* (1880), and with Flordeneu, queen of the Pyrenean faeries, in *Canigó*. Casals (2011b, 2-24) notes how Maragall, in letters to close friends such as Antoni Roura (1860–1910), referred to Clara as "the fairy," noting also the likely influence of Lord Byron's *Childe Harold's Pilgrimmage* (1814, 7th ed.). Separately, this is most likely a further allusion to the legendary Pyrenean faeries of Verdaguerian description.

520–522: And she's given fruit: / Many times has she been blessed by God, / And sometimes twice: Maragall and Clara Noble had thirteen children, including twins Clara and Anna in 1899 (Moreta 2010, 479).

540–552: A single couplet opens once again Adalaisa's response (as in lines 458-459 above), but now the decasyllables are feminine in this return to fully rhyming verse throughout the stanza (and remainder of "Scholium"). The uncanny shift to enclosing rhyme echoes the Poet's previous deployment in lines 490-497, except that Adalaisa here alternates feminine and masculine decasyllables (the Poet's were all masculine). Strikingly, the shift to enclosing rhyme is signaled by a sole unpaired and unrhymed feminine decasyllable ending in *partera* ("[puerperal] mother")—underscoring Adalaisa's unfulfilled desire for motherhood.

553–568: The Poet's masterful depiction of childbirth mirrors and extends the elaborate *aabccb* couplet/enclosing rhyme pattern throughout twelve decasyllables, yet tops off the stanza with a return to alternating feminine–masculine lines, spotlighting Adalaisa's removal from the world and the vanishing image of childbirth and, by extension, the renewal of life in the world.

569–578: Adalaisa's refusal to renounce life in the world while "the wanting in [her] senses rages on" culminates in her challenging the poet to re-empower her: "If you can't free me from [death's?] tyranny, / What good to you, then, poets, is your poetry?" The alternating feminine–masculine decasyllables will continue through to the end of "Scholium."

579–582: The Poet's brief reply completes the alternating rhyme of Adalaisa's point-blank question, yet Adalaisa's retort replaces the Poet's, reinstating her own alternating rhyme; deployment which underscores her dissatisfaction with the Poet's response.

583–594: Adalaisa's and the Poet's final remarks bring "Scholium," and with it, part two of *El comte Arnau* to a decisive yet open-ended conclusion in which silence is recommended by both, albeit for different reasons—she, unconvinced of his powers; he, hopeful of future poetic occasions. These concluding remarks are adroitly delivered by each of the two characters, respectively, in masculine–feminine decasyllables of recurring alternate *ababab* and *cdcdcd* rhyme, a prosodical tour de force that brings both the poem *El comte Arnau (part two)* and the volume *Enllà* to a remarkable end.

THE BEECH WOODS OF JORDÀ

Casals (1998, 749) dates the poem 18–19 October 1908. Its all-masculine decasyllables feature alternating *a*-sounding and *o*-sounding rhymed couplets, predominantly, with a single *u*-rhyming couplet (lines 9–10). The actual beech woods, La Fageda d'en Jordà, are located in the Garrotxa Volcanic Zone Natural Park, southeast of Olot, where Maragall would spend part of the summer (see headnote to *Seqüències*).

1: Abrams (2010, 401) points out the first line's allusion to the opening line of the poem "Mignon": "Kennst du das Land, wo die Zitronen blühn?" (from Goethe's *Wilhelm Meister's Apprenticeship*), which Maragall had translated into Catalan: "Saps el país dels tarongers en flor?" (*Les disperses*, 1904).

9–12: The single *u*-rhyming couplet (9–10) seems to underscore the fusion of the surrounding *stillness* ("quietud") and the walker who at this point becomes *lost* ("perdut"). Restated in the couplet following, the "sweet oblivion of the world" (11) stems from "the silence that governs that deep spot" (12).

13–16: In contrast to the elusive "freedom of the peaks" and ensuing sense of dread (see "Return"), the walker's sensation of being held "captive to silence and green" points—paradoxically—to a sensation of freedom within reach. The final line proves all the more forceful for its twofold exclamatory antithesis: "This fellowship [in solitude]!" and "This liberating prison!"

THE SIREN (FRAGMENT)

Casals (1998, 768) dates the poem between 1902 and 1904 (see head-note). The Catalan features mainly alternating feminine–masculine fully rhyming decasyllables, with significant variation in the opening and closing lines (see below). It has been remarked that the subtitle "fragment" may suggest a sense of incompletion in the social sense, that is, in the lives of the city's denizens (anticipating the social pathos in "New Ode to Barcelona"), rather than in the concrete sense of the poem as an unfinished piece (see Abrams 2010,

408-409); this alternate reading of "fragment" mirrors the polysemy at work in the lexeme "siren" (see below).

1–5: The sharp contrast between the beginning of the natural or celestial day—bringing "light reborn"—and the earthly day of "darkness" and its "scorching whistle" is signposted by the formal break between lines 2 and 3, followed by the unequivocal depiction and decrial of social injustice as the "tainted siren / calls the poor to work" (lines 4–5).

6–25: The poet shifts tone here to address the siren directly, detailing the worldly iniquity of the cityscape symbolized and sustained by the siren. Note how the polysemic quality of "siren" ("sirena") adds mythic muscle to the poem's imagery (lines 6–9).

26–30: The disrupted rhyme scheme underscores the disrupted lives of the poor as the poem's concluding statement addresses once again the reader (not the siren). The masculine verse featuring end rhyme with "assegut" (line 26) breaks the overall feminine–masculine pattern, creating an orphan couplet straddling the poem's disjointed addressees (siren–reader); the seemingly mismatched, unrhymed tandem "casa" (house) / "estrany" (strange), in lines 27 and 29, uncannily packages and delivers the full force of the estrangement, prevailing on the cityscape, that has now invaded the home.

NEW ODE TO BARCELONA

The first twenty-five lines of the poem are dated 4 February 1909, prior to the profound social strife concomitant to the Tragic Week (July 26-31, 1909) and the repression following in its wake; the remainder (lines 26–100) was composed subsequently (see headnote). The prosodic contrast between the pre- and post-Tragic Week sections signposts the enormity of the social crisis.

1–25: The prosody in this section calques fairly closely the Catalan alexandrines of Verdaguer's "A Barcelona" ("To Barcelona"), though Maragall diverges from Verdaguer particularly in his end rhyme, preferring assonant to perfect rhyme, or no rhyme, and varying freely masculine–feminine hemistichs at the caesura.

1–8: Maragall is quick to equate Barcelona with Catalonia, reaffirming and underscoring Barcelona's role as the country's driving and unifying spirit. This spirit, having moved outward beyond the city's former walls and taken hold of its mountains, embodies freedom (in contraposition to the various sets of walls restricting its movement that have now been superseded). Where to now? The city's reply is unequivocal: move further outward, and onward, to assume its role as the dynamic core of the larger natural and human geography designated Catalonia. Remarkably striking and important is the occurrence of the word "love" (line 7): the very thing that Maragall will later define as the "primary social reason" and whose absence Maragall will decry in "Ah! Barcelona..." (see headnote to "Ah! Barcelona..." in the prose section of this selection).

18: Its ranging peaks: The Pyrenees.

21–22: This second occurrence of "love"—again voiced by the city— very near the end of this pre-July section of the poem infuses the process of the city's expanding presence throughout Catalonia.

25–28: Stretch far, stretch far (line 25): This final image of the pre-July section depicts an expanding Barcelona/Catalonia that thrives under the auspices of "the primary social reason," that is, the Christian-inspired and public-spirited love that will soon prove to be lacking (line 28; again, see headnote to "Ah! Barcelona…"). Maragall marks the turning point in the poem somewhat subtly at first, completing the unfinished quatrain (lines 26–28). The rhetorical straw-man gambit (lines 27–28) exposes the city's fatal "lacking" (contrasting, on closer examination, with the "love" of the previous stanza) by way of a direct and unsparing matter-of-fact recrimination. As for the prosody, scansion reveals that the final two lines of the Catalan quatrain feature hendecasyllables (6 + 5 / 6 + 5), spotlighting the poet's stark statement and throwing into relief the city's unfortunate "lacking."

29–34: Now shunning all pretense of conventional prosodic formality, the poet's decrial shapeshifts to accommodate its new disruptive tenor and remonstrative content. You're a coward, you're cruel (line 29): This is the poem's first general reference to the Tragic Week and its sequel: the cowardly and cruel executions of Francesc Ferrer i Guàrdia (see headnote) and four others, and perhaps also to those whose inaction fanned the violence that last week in July. There shines a bright sky (line 31): The image of the bright sky—contrasting with Barcelona's true character—will return near the end of the poem (lines 81–85).

50–53: The muse and the nymph and the lady and the nun (line 50): This is the first specific reference to the Tragic Week, and caricature of Barcelona's womanly avatars.

55–64: This is one of the poem's hardest hitting stanzas. The sudden and treacherous violence that is coupled with boisterous laughter evokes the earlier poem "Paternal" ("Fatherhood") (see headnote to *Poesies* and endnotes to "Fatherhood"). This stanza features three generic signifiers—"mountain," "castle," and "ribs"—that denote specific places of importance with respect to the violence that took hold of the city: the mountain of Montjuïc and its fortress or "castle," military prison and site of summary tribunals and several executions, and the "ribs" or flanks denoting the Ronda Sant Antoni and the Avinguda Paral·lel, where confrontations were especially violent during the week of the fatal uprising (Casals 1998, 790, n. 64).

65–73: This stanza antithetically juxtaposes the two Ramblas: the one "a thing of beauty" (line 65) (that is, the well-to-do sectors of La Rambla dels Estudis, La Rambla de les Flors, and La Rambla dels Caputxins); and the other (La Rambla de Santa Mònica) "fevering for scraps" (line 71) (see Abrams 2010, 442).

86–94: In this penultimate stanza there appears the temple that "blooms gigantic, flowerlike" (line 87). Again, curiously, the Holy Family Temple—just as previous important places in the poem—is denoted generically, not by its proper name. The appearance of the temple in the poem is decisive: holding out future promise for those who are, or are to be, the faithful. Rising and thriving, the temple anticipates a rising and thriving people to come—and it is, significantly, an expiatory temple; that is, it can empower the faithful with atonement and reconciliation. Contextualizing more particularly here the role of the symbol of the Holy Family, we might also note how the growing social and moral crises of the early- and mid-nineteenth century had given impetus to the founding of Catholic associations in France and Belgium that would seek to fortify devotion to the Holy Family, holding it up as a model for working-class families in danger of falling victim to the spiritual and moral decay rampant amid the Industrial Revolution. Joaquim Molas (2003, 567) reminds us of Hector Berlioz' (1803-1869) sacred trilogy oratorio *L'Enfance du Christ* (1853-1854); and Ricard Torrents (2006) has examined at length the religious, aesthetic, and biographical affinities between Jacint Verdaguer (the *Jesús Infant* trilogy, 1890, 1891, 1893) and Antoni Gaudí (1852-1926), and how their devotion to the Holy Family sprung from this troubled context and, given their respective literary and architectural expression, how each sought to revitalize in the public spirit this powerful and important symbol. In short, the climactic appearance of the temple near the poem's end embodies hope for the public-spirited love that is lacking (see above), and the birth of a new temple suggests the birth of a new future, a new people. In Maragall's vision of conviviality, driven by love, "the primary social reason," the power of the temple's symbolism lies in its ability to once again help turn the population into a people.

95–100: Conclusively, the poem's final stanza—with the poet saying "I" for the first time (the interlocutor Barcelona, on the other hand, had replied in the first person to the poet's queries in stanzas two, four and six)—postulates the necessary condition for achieving reconciliation and conviviality as a people: recognition on the part of each individual "I" of the dangerously conflicting and potentially destructive elements that comprise the city and realization and acceptance also of each and everyone's own part in the whole. Note how the "I" (line 95) transitions to "us" (line 98) and "ours" (lines 99, 100) here as Maragall adroitly performs the recognition and acceptance of collective responsibility that is requisite to restoring conviviality in the wake of the Tragic Week. Beyond the sense of "ours" as indicating possession here, it is self-referential, floodlighting a "Barcelona" (lines 99, 100) of which all are part, and that needs to be put right by all; and yet, the remedy abides elusive so long as all remain powerless under the spell of the "Grand Enchantress" (line 100).

FROM *COUNT ARNAU* (PART THREE: THE END OF COUNT ARNAU)

The various parts of the poem are dated (with some degree of uncertainty) by Casals (1998, 793-800, 807) as follows: Verses 1-8: 22 August 1907; v. 17-24: between November 1908 and 4 February 1909; v. 25-28: January 1910; v. 29-36: 28-29 August 1908; v. 37-88: August 1908; v. 89-92: between November 1908 and 4 February 1909; v. 93-96: January 1910; v. 97-128: 25-26 August 1909; v. 129-160: January 1910. Reduced to four periods, the first three were composed during summer sojourns in Olot, and the last one in Barcelona. Maragall deploys octosyllables throughout, invariably, in fully rhyming, alternating feminine–masculine verses.

97–100: All the voices of the earth: These are the same voices that mocked Arnau when he at first failed to seduce Adalaisa, then showered praise on him at his subsequent success, and finally, mock and torment him along his endless ride. Arnau sees and passes among the living, but cannot be seen, numbering neither among the living nor spirits of the dead, "as in a dream, like a shadow, / as if awake among the sleeping" (lines 47–48; not included in this selection).

113–114: Meanwhile his wife spins and sings: Arnau converses with the spirit of his deceased wife Elvira (part two), who continues spinning and singing as she had done at home in Arnau's absence. She sings the love she felt for Arnau, by whom she feels betrayed: "I sing only the love I felt for you, / not the one you felt for me" (part two, lines 276–277; not included in this selection); to which Arnau replies: "Sing, wife, spin and sing, / and ease my suffering! / When wife sings and spins, / the home sleeps in peace" (lines 278–281).

121: It's a voice that is still living: Maragall's notion of what he calls "la paraula viva" (the living word), so central to his poetics, is explained clearly in his 1903 lecture *Elogi de la paraula* (In Praise of Words) (see the introduction to this volume).

136: And she's redeemed the one who sinned: Arnau had voiced his desire for redemption with the appearance of the traditional song (part two); his weeping had revealed to him his soul, which is the traditional song, following which he asks: "Will there be no redemption for a lost soul?" (line 232, part two)

159–160: On the significance and role of a "living voice" in the long-awaited redemption, see above (note to line 121) and the headnote to *Seqüències*.

SPIRITUAL

Casals (1998, 813, 815) dates the composition of the poem as follows: Verses 1-36: November 1909; v. 37-40: January 1910; v. 41-45: 4 February 1910. Maragall's prosody in what is widely considered to be his poetic masterpiece features decasyllables throughout, and weaves a complex interplay of, for the most part, fully rhyming feminine and masculine verses interposed variously in several stanzas, resulting in an elaborate, lyrical tableau tailored to the gravity and vitality of the poet's existential query.

1–3: In his insightful study, Josep Manuel Udina (2009)—for whom the poem stands as a model of philosophical inquiry—is quick to point out that the interpellator who queries the Lord is a believer, but one who also harbors doubt and seeks answers to the contradictory immanence–transcendence dichotomy (143); moreover, the form the poem takes is that of a prayer (147): this is the first (line 1) of six occurrences of the name "Lord" throughout the poem.

4: This face: Compare the vital image of the face in Maragall's early poem "Wedded" (line 70): "the indelible etchings of friends' faces."

5–6: The prominent entrance of the poem's first masculine rhyme "cor" (heart) / "mort" (death) is spotlighted by their reoccurrence ("death" in line 13, and both "heart" and "death" once again in lines 16–17), underscoring the difficulty of reconciling the worldly feeling of aliveness with the transcendent life postulated by religious faith. Stirring inside nonstop (line 6): Compare this image with the unending stir of life's waters in "Excelsior" (lines 11–12).

7–9: Maragall's disarmingly simple lexical choices—"sky," "mountains," "sea" and "sun"—evoke numerous other poems that put these simple words to powerful use in the poet's encounter with nature and life.

10–11: This statement echoes Arnau's (*Count Arnau*, 1, III, lines 35–36): "The only delight the heavens bring me / is when spread out above me over the earth."

12–16: The Faustian reference here is examined by Abrams (2010, 460-462), who points out that Faust is a counterpoint to Maragall: Faust's wager is not to say, "Stop!" to any moment, whereas the poet "would gladly / stop so many moments every day / and have them go on forever in my heart!" Terry weighs in significantly here, signposting the moment in Maragall's posthumous play *Nausica* (Nausicaa) in which the blind poet Daimó turns Nausicaa away from stopping her life at Ulysses's departure: "this would be a living death […] she must allow her experience to become memory, which, through its poetry and nobility, will enrich her life. Memory, in other words, no longer conflicts with further action, and the [Faustian] dilemma which troubles Maragall in the third stanza of the 'Cant espiritual' is resolved" (2001, 18-19).

25–27: Compare this statement to the concluding line of "Sunstruck":

"I come to bring the heavens nearer the earth..." (Note: the Catalan "pàtria" translates as "home" in its two occurrences here.)

28–31: Udina (2009, 142) poignantly suggests that the title of the poem might just as well be "Worldly Song" or "Song Both Worldly and Spiritual."

32–45: Udina formulates concisely: the poem features "the simultaneous presence of a transcendent dimension (of faith and prayer), and the stubborn affirmation of immanence (of this world and its beauty, and the senses and the body): simultaneity of an immanence and a transcendence that the author desires to be one and the same thing" (147). This dovetails, as noted previously by Terry (2001, 19), with the dictum Maragall put forth in an article titled "La panacea" written shortly before his death: "Try to use the body as a soul and the soul as a body" (in *Diario de Barcelona*, 16 Nov. 1911).

REFERENCES

Abrams, D. Sam. 2010. *Llegir Maragall, ara.* Barcelona: Proa.

Albert, Caterina. 1903. Letter to Joan Maragall, 12-16 May 1903. In "Aplec de correspondència rebuda de Víctor Català, de 26 cartes compreses entre els anys 1902 a 1911." Fons Personal de Joan Maragall. Biblioteca de Catalunya.

———. (1898) 2018. "The Infanticide." In *Silent Souls and Other Stories*, edited and translated by Kathleen McNerney. New York: Modern Language Association. (Originally published as "La infanticida.")

Ardolino, Francesco. 2006. *Una literatura entre el dogma i l'heretgia: les influències de Dante en l'obra de Joan Maragall.* Barcelona: Cruïlla / Fundació Joan Maragall.

Benet, Josep. *Maragall i la Setmana Tràgica* (1963) 2009. Barcelona: Edicions 62.

Bush, Peter. 2006. "The writer of translations." In *The Translator as Writer*, edited by Susan Bassnett and Peter Bush. London: Continuum, 23-32.

Byron, George Gordon, Lord. 1822. *Cain: A mystery*. London: H. Gray.

Capote, Truman. [1958] 1993. *Breakfast at Tiffany's*. New York: Vintage Books.

Casals, Glòria, ed. 1998. *Joan Maragall: Poesia: Edició crítica*. Barcelona: Edicions de la Magrana.

———. 2011a. "Dones de Maragall: a propòsit de Clara i Haidé." In *Joan Maragall, paraula i pensament*, edited by Josep-Maria Terricabras. Girona: Publicacions de la Càtedra Ferrater Mora, 37-69.

———, ed. 2011b. *Joan Maragall – Clara Noble: Cartes de festeig*. Girona: Edicions de la Ela Geminada.

Casasses, Enric. 2014. *Intent de comentar-hi el poema d'en Joan Maragall "Soleiada."* Bellcaire d'Empordà: Edicions Vitel·la.

Laín Entralgo, Pedro. 1960, 1961, 1981. "Pròleg." In *Obres completes*, Joan Maragall, vol. 2. Editorial Selecta, 14-31.

Lluís Font, Pere. 2009. "Maragall davant la Setmana Tràgica." *Serra d'Or* 593, 25-28.

Maragall, Joan. (1900) 1961, 1981. "La Escuadra del Almirante Cervera." In *Obres completes*, vol. 2. Barcelona: Editorial Selecta, 590-594.

———. (1903a) 1960, 1970, 1981. "A Víctor Català." In *Obres completes*, vol. 1. Barcelona: Editorial Selecta, 942-943.

———. (1903b) 1960, 1970, 1981. "Elogi de la paraula." In *Obres completes*, vol. 1. Barcelona: Editorial Selecta, 663-668.

———. (1903c) 1961, 1981. Letter to Felip Pedrell (29 Oct. 1903). In

Obres completes, vol. 2. Barcelona: Editorial Selecta, 924.

———. (1904a) 1960, 1970, 1981. "Advertència del traductor" preceding La Margarideta. In *Obres completes*, vol. 1. Barcelona: Editorial Selecta, 274-276.

———. (1904b) 2010. "Als amics de *Joventut*" preceding *Les disperses*. In *Joan Maragall: Poesia completa*, edited by Glòria Casals and Lluís Quintana. Barcelona: Edicions 62, 109-110.

———. (1911a) 1960, 1970, 1981. Letter to Carles Rahola (23 Jan. 1911). In *Obres completes*, vol. 1. Barcelona: Editorial Selecta, 1081-1082.

———. (1911b) 1961, 1981. Letter to Lluís Lluís (20 Feb. 1911). In *Obres completes*, vol. 2. Barcelona: Editorial Selecta, 914.

———. 1960, 1970, 1981. *Obres completes*, vol. 1. Barcelona: Editorial Selecta.

Marfany, Joan-Lluís. 1986. "Joan Maragall." In *Història de la literatura catalana*, vol. 8, edited by Martí de Riquer, Antoni Comas and Joaquim Molas. Barcelona: Ariel.

Molas, Joaquim. 2003. Introduction to "Jesús Infant." In *Poemes llargs/ Teatre*. Vol. II. *Totes les obres de Jacint Verdaguer*, edited by Joaquim Molas and Isidor Cònsul. Barcelona: Proa, 567-569.

Moreta, Ignasi. 2010. *No et facis posar cendra: pensament i religió en Joan Maragall*. Barcelona: Fragmenta Editorial.

Muñoz i Pairet, Irene. 2015. "Joan Maragall i Víctor Català, des del seu epistolari." *Haidé: Estudis maragallians* 4, 41-51.

Parcerisas, Francesc. 2012. "Epíleg: Cloenda de l'Any Maragall." In *En el batec del temps.* Barcelona: Institució de les Lletres Catalanes / Associació Família de Joan Maragall i Clara Noble, 453-459.

Passola, Tònia. 2012. " 'Una veu encara viva,' Joan Maragall i la poesia popular." In *En el batec del temps.* Barcelona: Institució de les Lletres Catalanes / Associació Família de Joan Maragall i Clara Noble, 338-343.

Pijoan, Josep. (1927) 2010. *El meu don Joan Maragall.* Barcelona: Quaderns Crema.

Puppo, Ronald, ed., trans. 2007. *Selected Poems of Jacint Verdaguer: A Bilingual Edition*, with an introduction by Ramon Pinyol i Torrents. The University of Chicago Press.

———. 2012a. "How Maragall's notion of a public-spirited love resonates in English translation." *Haidé: Estudis maragallians* 1, 93-107.

———. 2012b. "The poetry of troubles: Maragall's *Els tres cants de la guerra (Three songs of war)* and their translation." *Journal of Catalan Studies* 14 (2011), 217-236.

———. 2016. "Contrast and Confluence in Verdaguer's and Maragall's Poetic Peopling of Barcelona." *Catalan Review* XXX, 87-109.

———. 2017. "The poetized peopling of nineteenth-century Spain/s." In *The Routledge Companion to Iberian Studies*, edited by Javier Muñoz-Basols, Laura Lonsdale and Manuel Delgado. London: Routledge, 344-356.

Quintana, Lluís. 1997. "Joan Maragall i el mite del comte Arnau." In *Quaderns Fundació Joan Maragall: Joan Maragall i el comte Arnau.* Barcelona: Editorial Claret, 5-18.

Quintana, Lluís, Jordi Castellanos, Susanna Rafart, and Pere Ballart.

2008. *Maragall, alguns poemes: lectures i comentaris d'autor*. Barcelona: Biblioteca de Catalunya.

Radigales, Jaume. 1997. "La relació epistolar entre Joan Maragall i Felip Pedrell a l'entorn d'*El comte Arnau*." In *Quaderns Fundació Joan Maragall: Joan Maragall i el comte Arnau*. Barcelona: Editorial Claret, 19-30.

Rafart, Susanna. See: Quintana *et al*. 2008.

Resina, Joan Ramon. 2009. "Post-Hispanism, or the long goodbye of National Philology." In *Writers In Between Languages: Minority Literatures in the Global Scene*, edited by Mari José Olaziregi. Reno: Center for Basque Studies/University of Nevada, 25-38.

Romeu i Figueras, Josep. (1963) 2000. "El mite del comte Arnau." In *Joan Maragall: El comte Arnau*, with introductory texts by Josep Romeu i Figueras, Arthur Terry and Joan-Lluís Marfany. Barcelona: Edicions 62, 7-15.

Schleiermacher, Friedrich. (1813) 2004. "On the Different Methods of Translating." In *The Translation Studies Reader* (2nd ed), edited by Lawrence Venuti. London: Routledge, 43-63.

Serrahima, Maurici. 1981. *Vida i obra de Joan Maragall*. Barcelona: Editorial Laia.

Solà, Lluís. 2012. "El lloc de la paraula." In *En el batec del temps*. Barcelona: Institució de les Lletres Catalanes / Associació Família de Joan Maragall i Clara Noble, 223-241.

———. 2013. *La paraula i el món: Assaigs sobre poesia*. Barcelona: L'Avenç.

Sotelo Vázquez, Adolfo. 2016. "Joan Maragall i l'aula de la Facultat de

Filologia." *Haidé: Estudis maragallians* 5, 81-84.

Spivak, Gayatri Chakravorty. 1993. "The politics of translation." In her *Outside in the Teaching Machine*. London: Routledge, 179-200.

Terricabras, Josep-Maria, ed. 2011. *Joan Maragall, paraula i pensament*. Girona: Publicacions de la Càtedra Ferrater Mora.

Terry, Arthur. (1963) 1999. *La poesia de Joan Maragall*. Barcelona: Quaderns Crema.

———. (1963) 2000. "La força de la poesia en *El comte Arnau*." In *Joan Maragall: El comte Arnau*, with introductory texts by Josep Romeu i Figueras, Arthur Terry and Joan-Lluís Marfany. Barcelona: Edicions 62, 17-38.

———. 2001. "The Poetry of Joan Maragall." The Annual Joan Gili Memorial Lecture delivered at the Palau de la Generalitat during the Anglo-Catalan Society's XLVI Annual Conference, Barcelona, 14-17 December, 2000. Sheffield: The Hallamshire Press Limited.

———. 2003. *A Companion to Catalan Literature*. Woodbridge: Tamesis.

Torrents, Ricard. 2003. Introduction to Canigó. In *Poems llargs/Teatre*, vol. 2 of *Totes les obres de Jacint Verdaguer*, edited by Joaquim Molas and Isidor Cònsul. Barcelona: Proa, 241-245.

———. 2006. *Art, poder i religió: La Sagrada Família en Verdaguer i Gaudí*. Barcelona: Proa.

———. 2011. "Maragall i Gorina, Joan." In *Diccionari de la traducció catalana*, edited by Montserrat Bacardí and Pilar Godayol. Vic: Eumo Editorial, 314-316.

Udina, Josep Manuel. 2009. "Una lectura no canònica del *Cant espiritual* de Joan Maragall." *Enrahonar* 42, 141-149.

Venuti, Lawrence. 2009. Introduction to *Edward Hopper Poems*, by Ernest Farrés, xi-xix. Translated by Lawrence Venuti. Minneapolis: Graywolf Press. (Originally published as *Edward Hopper: Cinquanta poemes sobre la seva obra pictòrica*. Barcelona: Viena Edicions, 2006.)

Verdaguer, Jacint. 2007. *Selected Poems of Jacint Verdaguer: A Bilingual Edition*, edited and translated by Ronald Puppo, with an introduction by Ramon Pinyol i Torrents. Univeristy of Chicago Press.

———. [1886] 2015. *Mount Canigó: A tale of Catalonia*, edited and translated by Ronald Puppo. Barcelona/Woodbridge: Barcino/Tamesis.

INDEX OF TITLES AND FIRST LINES